"From homeownership to relationships to parenthood, Carmen knows that money is about so much more than numbers. This book will help you make real-world financial decisions—and improve your life."

—Kimberly Palmer, author of *Generation Earn* and
personal finance columnist at *U.S. News & World Report*

"The Real Cost of Living is a great framework for telling the story of money. Carmen combines her knack for getting to the heart of the matter with the butt-kicking spirit of a personal trainer. Readers will get their financial lives in shape."

—Bob Sullivan, writer of MSNBC.com's Red Tape Chronicles and
author of the *New York Times* bestsellers *Gotcha Capitalism* and
Stop Getting Ripped Off

WITHDRAWN

"Most financial planning books promise big returns without mentioning risk. Carmen Wong Ulrich takes a more useful—and practical—approach by discussing costs. She understands lower costs correlate with higher returns. I highly recommend her book."

—Daniel R. Solin, author of the bestselling *The Smartest Investment Book You'll
Ever Read, The Smartest 401(k) Book You'll Ever Read,*
and *The Smartest Retirement Book You'll Ever Read*

"This book is a tool that we all should use as we build a better life."

—Joi Gordon, CEO of Dress for Success Worldwide

continued ...

"*The Real Cost of Living* is a must-read for everyone of every age. Because of Carmen's training in psychology and her varied life experiences, she sees the world of personal finance through an entirely unique lens. This is no 'ordinary' money book. Carmen invites the reader to examine and reflect on why we make the choices we do as we explore how each choice has a personal as well as a financial cost and reward. As she deftly points out, *everything* has a cost attached to it; things we think about and things we never thought we had to think about are discussed from the perspective of choice. Ms. Wong Ulrich explains the real cost of living with depth and humor, peppered with superb relatable examples. This is a handbook to help us make important life choices so we can be aware of living our lives consciously, realistically, and responsibly."

—Dale V. Atkins, PhD, psychologist, relationship expert, and author of *Sanity Savers*

PRAISE FOR CARMEN WONG ULRICH

"Ulrich's advice is simple and to the point . . . (She) does argue for some big nationwide initiatives, like a higher minimum wage and increased credit card regulation, but she's much more concerned with providing basic solutions to individual financial crises—and delivers the goods effectively." —*Publishers Weekly*

"Rich with commonsense insights and easy-to-implement plans . . . *Generation Debt* brings a critically important topic to life in a helpful, fun package." —Robert Safian, editor in chief of *Fast Company* magazine

THE
Real Cost of Living

Making the Best Choices for You, Your Life, and Your Money

Carmen Wong Ulrich

A PERIGEE BOOK

A PERIGEE BOOK
Published by the Penguin Group
Penguin Group (USA) Inc.
375 Hudson Street, New York, New York 10014, USA
Penguin Group (Canada), 90 Eglinton Avenue East, Suite 700, Toronto, Ontario M4P 2Y3, Canada
(a division of Pearson Penguin Canada Inc.)
Penguin Books Ltd., 80 Strand, London WC2R 0RL, England
Penguin Group Ireland, 25 St. Stephen's Green, Dublin 2, Ireland (a division of Penguin Books Ltd.)
Penguin Group (Australia), 250 Camberwell Road, Camberwell, Victoria 3124, Australia
(a division of Pearson Australia Group Pty. Ltd.)
Penguin Books India Pvt. Ltd., 11 Community Centre, Panchsheel Park, New Delhi—110 017, India
Penguin Group (NZ), 67 Apollo Drive, Rosedale, North Shore 0632, New Zealand
(a division of Pearson New Zealand Ltd.)
Penguin Books (South Africa) (Pty.) Ltd., 24 Sturdee Avenue, Rosebank, Johannesburg 2196, South Africa
Penguin Books Ltd., Registered Offices: 80 Strand, London WC2R 0RL, England

First edition: January 2011

Library of Congress Cataloging-in-Publication Data

Ulrich, Carmen Wong.
    The real cost of living : making the best choices for you, your life, and your money / Carmen Wong
Ulrich.
    p.   cm.
    "A Perigee book."
    Includes index.
    ISBN 978-0-399-53644-1
    1. Finance, Personal.   2. Finance, Personal—Psychological aspects.   I. Title.
    HG179.U423 2011
    332.024—dc22   2010035980

PRINTED IN THE UNITED STATES OF AMERICA

10   9   8   7   6   5   4   3   2   1

For Bianca, who is priceless.

CONTENTS

INTRODUCTION

We had just gotten back from a rainy run to our local Target, toddler in tow. Bad traffic, chilly wet weather, and a grumpy two-year-old had us happy to hoist our haul back home and settle in for the remainder of the afternoon.

"Oh, man! It's ripped!" My husband let flow his outrage at our brand-new, out-of-package, torn mattress cover. "That's it," he grumbled as he rolled it back up. "I'm going back."

"In that mess?! It'll take two hours there and back, not to mention the lines." I saw no reason to renew a rendezvous with rain, traffic, and customer service for a $7.99 mattress cover.

I managed to talk him out of heading back into a hostile Sunday afternoon at the shopping center but only after I expressed why I thought his time may be better spent with us. He felt that it was worthwhile to go back because of the principle of the matter, not the money. We were sold a bad piece of merchandise—a manufacturing accident, surely—and he wanted the vendor to know. It was good customer service. I, on the other hand, felt that it was all about how much our time was worth—at that point, a lot more than $7.99. Instead of him traveling back to the store, he could watch the baby so I could get dinner started. We could then enjoy dinner at a regular hour, keeping the baby on the schedule that seemed to make her happy and then bedtime at a good hour would ensue. Time lost to getting that $7.99 back (or a new, functioning mattress cover) was a domino effect to me: lost time, lost money, lost nerves due to a baby thrown off schedule. Granted, it's a privilege that we had a choice: the $7.99 or the two hours. But it was a choice nonetheless. Only one choice of dozens that we make on a weekly basis that sometimes have to do with money but sometimes have less to do with money than with what we want: happiness, security, peace in the house. Because my degrees are not in finance but in psychology, and my experience and training is in journalism, throughout my career in personal finance I have seen and continue to see money differently from those trained in the more technical side of the profession. On the personal finance show I hosted and coproduced for CNBC for a year, *On the Money*, I was able to not only report and research personal finance but to interact with you, viewers and readers, at a level few journalists experience. Through the show, as well as on Facebook and Twitter, I'd communicate with as many people as possible to not only help with money questions and conundrums but to learn more about what was vexing you about financial decisions—and life—in general (it was the best part of my job). This happened at a heady time—the Great Recession that began in 2008. A time when help, knowledge, and guidance about money was needed more than ever.

But I noticed that what was needed just as much as facts, websites, and strategy was understanding.

I saw the psychological costs of financial decisions take their toll growing up. I know how defeating it can feel to not be able to get out of debt. And we all know how important insurance and a will are, but sometimes we just put these things off. Why? Because what we do with money sometimes isn't about money. Economics has finally recognized that we are not rational creatures; we're not all about the accounting. Behavioral economics, the study of the neuropsychology behind how we behave with our money, has won Nobel Prizes. But it's also time—especially for those of us in personal finance—to realize that there is a lot more going on than money when it comes to making decisions about our money and our lives.

On the show, sometimes a panel of financial planners would come on to take callers' questions with me. Once in a while, I'd be amazed at how one would pontificate on why he was right (they were mostly he's) and off camera, how "stupid" people could be, when it wasn't stupidity guiding the caller's decision but a personal need. Of course, when I disagreed with these planners, I let them and everyone watching know, but there were few times when a planner would realize why the caller or guest was just not getting it: because the planner wasn't listening to *why* the viewers were doing what they were doing. Why does this caller insist on prepaying her mortgage? Because she saw her mother lose her home to the bank and she doesn't ever want that to happen to her. Why does this couple think it's okay to have such a big, expensive car? Because they grew up poor, work too hard, don't have time to enjoy the results, and the car is not only a symbol of what they're working toward but something they can take pleasure in day in and day out. (I still told that couple to get rid of the car, but they were receptive to that advice only after I listened to them talk about what the car symbolized and acknowledged their motivation.) Why does this man want to use up his life savings to pay for his son's college tuition? Because education is his American Dream, and he knows that his son will care for him in his old age. Why does this woman smoke two packs a day when she can barely pay her bills? Because she's hooked and needs help.

Barking orders is not my style. I am in the business of changing behavior, and lives, for the better. And I know that you are more likely to change your behavior if someone respects and recognizes where you're coming from—your motivations, your needs, your fears, and your dreams—then explains your options. I respect that we all have needs that go beyond the bottom line on a balance sheet. (But to be clear, my bark will come out if you are doing something terribly detrimental to your financial life and the lives of your family.) Outside of that, personal finance is not only about returns, interest rates, and insurance. Changing behavior means acknowledging that there are factors beyond money that influence how you spend, save, and make plans for your money.

Ask yourself when you're about to make a financial decision, which could be as mundane as shopping online to as pressing as choosing life insurance: *What is nudging me in that direction right now? What am I feeling? Is that my dad's voice in my head? What will people think?* Then stop to listen: *This makes me anxious. I want to be secure. I shop when I'm bored. I don't like math.* Listening to that inner voice is the companion to this book.

This book is about how to help you make better choices in life. Choices that sometimes seem to be all about money, but probably aren't, as well as choices that seem to have nothing to do with money, but should be all about the dollah bills, y'all. We all want to make better decisions in life, decisions that make us happy personally as well as financially. And many decisions have personal costs as well as financial costs.

You know the old "make a list of pros and cons" tactic? It's a helpful technique that clarifies the potential outcomes of a choice and helps you understand and weigh your options more clearly. Think of this book as Pro/Con 4.0. It's not so much about bad choices vs. good choices as it is a way to help you lay out all the factors to take into consideration before you make any moves with your money.

My brainy sister fact-checked this book. I didn't ask for any particular feedback, just, "What'd ya think?" Her answer: "There are a lot of things in there that I've just never thought of!" I hope that's your reaction to this book, too. And that you'll take those things and use them when you're making decisions. You'll be more likely to make the best choices.

The Real Cost of
Home

Home is where the heart is,
but it's also where risk lives.

How would it feel to lose $400,000?

Imagine: You're not a millionaire. In fact, this was your life's savings. Victims of Bernie Madoff and other schemers can relate. But what if the culprit, the villain, were not some evil, greedy scammer, but your home?

The Great Recession was a robber in many ways. Though many of us saw billions disappear in our retirement accounts invested in the stock market, we then saw those holdings recover a bit. But for most of the country, the loss of value in our homes and the incredibly slow recovery was a theft with no one to arrest (well, almost no one). At one point in 2009, 81 percent of all homes in Las Vegas, Nevada, were underwater—meaning the majority of owners owed more on their mortgages than their homes were worth; in reality they owned nothing.

What happened to the American Dream? We learned—the hard

way—what we should have known all along. Owning a home is not only a dream, but a reality. A reality that makes you part of a market, just like any other market, like stocks or bonds. The emotions and attachments we have with our homes can fall prey to things completely out of our control: the housing market and overall economy. The scariest part is that we've never lived to see anything like the most recent housing collapse before.

The first home my mother owned in this country was a four-bedroom railroad apartment in West Harlem, New York. When we later moved to New England, her parents, my grandparents, moved into the apartment and became the owners. Over thirty years, the value of the home went from around $40,000 to $90,000. Not so good a return. So, after both my grandmother and grandfather passed away, why not sell what wasn't turning out to be such a good investment? It was 1991 and $90,000 seemed fair. Fast-forward to 1998 and there's roots-craving me, back in the city, thinking that maybe now, with a few years of postcollege work and good credit under my belt, I could buy the old apartment back. I loved the building and loved the neighborhood, and a lot had changed since the crack-filled 1980s. I got an amazing wake-up call. The apartment was now worth nearly *eight times* more. How did a home that barely budged in value over thirty years end up exploding in value in only seven years?

The ten to fifteen years leading to 2007 were some of the most astronomical, purple-elephant years of growth the American real estate market had ever seen. Homes were pumped up like stocks, bloated with phantom value (unless you sold). But we and my grandparents didn't live in a stock. We lived in a home.

. . .

And as for that $400,000? Michael was a lively, handsome guy who did pretty well for himself, well enough to buy his mom a home. But it was his own home he was worried about. In a move to secure the best interest rate on his mortgage as well as lower the amount he had to borrow, to make the home fully his sooner, Michael had put his life savings of $400,000 (cash!) down on his West Coast home, which was valued at the time (2007) at $800,000. He really thought it was the right thing to do—after all, if you're planning to stay put for a while, isn't paying off your mortgage early a great financial move? Sometimes, but not this time. Michael called my show because he didn't know what to do: His home was now worth only $400,000. Michael had lost *half* the value of his home, and the cold, hard reality was that by putting so much cash up front, he had bet *his* money, not the bank's money, on the value of his home always going up. It was a gamble that cost him his life savings. But what if he stayed in the home for twenty or thirty years; wouldn't he get his money back in equity as his home value went up? Sounds like too much of a long-term investment to me: twenty to thirty years to wait and *maybe* get his original investment back, and no gains. The worst part is, it didn't have to be that way.

But it's not all about the money.

OUR HOMES ARE PERSONAL

A dear friend of mine told me recently of an old friend whose husband had just died. She'd taken all of the insurance money and paid off the mortgage on the home they lived in together, even though her money would have better served her someplace else. When asked why she did this, the new widow responded, "Because it's all I have. I have to keep it." What she really meant was it's all she has left of him and the memories of their life together. She didn't want the bank or the economy or her job situation to be able to take away the home she had raised a family in with her husband. She made a big financial decision with a tremendous personal benefit, rather than a financial one. She needed security. She wanted her memories intact. The cost? Thousands of dollars in possible unrealized gains from investing the money elsewhere. But the financial cost was well worth it to her for the personal benefits of priceless memories and solace.

We all know the feeling of relief (or at least I hope you do) of coming home after being away for a business trip, vacation, or even just after a long, hard day. Our homes may be structures that we rent or own, but their biggest, most immediate personal value is the shelter they provide. A roof over our heads, a place to grow a family, a respite from hard work. The benefit of having and enjoying shelter of our own is nearly priceless even if like me in my first apartment you've got only a shower stall made of plastic. (At least I had hot water . . . most of the time.) Shelter is a primal human, even animal, need, but our homes are not only a place to go when we need to sleep; we load our homes with much more in terms of who we are and how we feel.

Wrapped up in our identity as Americans is the idea that what we do and where we live compose a large part of who we are as people—our values, our "tribe," our political leanings, our food, frames of reference, and so on. Second only to our jobs in terms of identity we can place our homes, where we choose to live and how we live within it. Many of us also wrap this up in the idea of the American Dream: *I'm going to retire to a condo in Boca. All I want is a nice colonial with a yard for the kids and a nice school. If I leave the city, I'll just die. Not in my backyard!* Our homes, like our cars, can be an outward reflection of who we are, where we are in our lives and our aspirations.

You already may feel kinship with a neighbor because you live in the same area, you share a certain space, but if you walk in and onto piles of dust bunnies, toys, and mayhem, your feelings of kinship may change. You judge that person as messy, maybe lazy, maybe too busy, maybe ill. The next day you meet a new friend at an event. You really get along and seem to have similar interests. Then, she tells you that she lives in Greenwich (Connecticut, one of the richest towns in the country) while you live in Washington Heights (New York, one of the less wealthy neighborhoods in Manhattan). So you both make an instant assessment: She's too rich to know at all what my life is like, or her life is too different from mine. So, nice to meet you! As you may go your separate ways.

I hope we're all more open minded than that but even if you did remain friends and in contact, the initial judgment exists. This is called *place identity.* The idea that where we are is part of who we are. And when you lose your home or can't save or make enough to get the home you want or think you deserve, you suffer personally—your identity takes a hit. And as our identities are so tied to our jobs, they are tied as well to our ZIP codes and how we decorate and manage our homes, our space. So where we choose to live and how can determine much of our levels of happiness, fulfillment, and feelings of success and accomplishment.

Why did so many people buy too much house before the recession? Because who doesn't want a bigger, better house? It means I'm a bigger, better *me*! A flawed and inflated sense of self and a desire to attain the outward signs of the moneyed is a weakness many lenders were more than happy to exploit during the housing boom. After all, the average square footage of a home in 1973 was only 1,660, while in 2007 we hit an average high of 2,521. We ballooned our homes by almost half in size while our incomes remained nearly stagnant in the same period of time. I am thankful that our home size is shrinking again as many bloated McMansions are no longer affordable and as we become more aware of our environmental footprint (another cost). We're now down to an average closer to 2,400 square feet, and falling.

Place attachment also plays a factor in the personal cost of losing our homes. Losing your home due to illness or a layoff or even just having to relocate for a job that you can't afford to lose can feel soul crushing and speaks to just how much we value the places we live. If we lose our homes we can feel rootless, failed, humiliated, and even devastated. We get attached both in feeling and identity.

Strangely enough, over several decades we've become an incredibly mobile nation; key here is upwardly mobile. By 2007, the height of the housing boom, 38.7 million of us moved from one home to another. But it seems like we like to move when times are flush (bigger homes, better neighborhoods) but we stop moving when things get rocky; by 2008 Americans were moving at the lowest rate since 1943! Hunker down, stay home, hold tight.

Buying a home also ties us down not only financially but personally to a structure that we need to maintain and cannot just walk away from (more on walking away soon). There is remarkable symbolism in owning a home with strong ties to our history in this country as well as international concepts of landowners vs. workers or renters. Owning a home projects to the rest of society (whether it's true or not) a particular sense of accomplishment, responsibility, and an implied investment in your neighborhood. You become part of a group of people who, you hope, care about their surroundings—since you own some space—and have settled down. You become part of a community whether you're active in it or not. Owning a home once meant that you were stable in your finances, your job, and your home life. With such housing drama during the most recent recession, our ideas of what owning means and projects have changed a bit, but only a bit. Our ideas and traditions remain ingrained, whether they're good for our wallets and lifestyle or not.

One day on a top morning show I disagreed (politely) with a fellow guest who was advising a young couple who were in the military to buy another home after they got rid of the one they had, even though they moved every three years due to their careers. My argument against that: They were stuck with a home, nearly underwater, because of a bad housing market and the need to move for their jobs. If they continued to buy a home every time they had to move (every three years), they would bankrupt themselves over time.

We ran out of time on the air but the other guest hadn't finished with me. He followed me back to the green room, incredulous: "So you're telling me that when I stand in front of a military audience that I should tell all of them to not buy a home, ever?!"

"If they're moving every three years or even five years or less, yes, that's exactly what I'm telling you."

Here was a situation where the American Dream of homeownership clashed with a lifestyle. Between closing costs, Realtor fees, legal fees, maintenance, taxes, not to mention what happens in the housing market, three years is not enough time to earn or even keep money that you put into buying and maintaining a home. And the couple was calling because they couldn't unload the house; they were stuck paying a mortgage, taxes, maintenance, and now rent in another city, *and* they lost some of their down payment to the falling housing market.

So why was this other guest so adamant and passionate about being able to tell even moving-military folks that they should buy a home, even if it made bad financial sense? Because it's the American Dream.

In tough times it's natural to search out security—things that make us feel anchored and in control. Owning our homes can be a salve for our fears about the unknown (such as the complicated and intimidating stock market) and our need to see where our money is going. But how much of this security benefit is a reality? This reality is fluid, because there are so many other costs in owning a home beyond the actual value of the property. Even if you own your home free and clear, do you have enough insurance? Are maintenance costs going to run you out? Are your property taxes as big as your former mortgage? Or, like Michael, the $400,000 Man, how much of your hard-earned dollars are you willing to lose to a fluctuating housing market? And for those of us who are still on the borrowing side of our mortgages, the bank owns our homes. How much security is there in ownership when there is so much that can go wrong?

To get to the nitty-gritty of the real cost of owning a home, there are a couple of big things that must be understood to get the reality of either owning or renting and what both actually cost.

- **Your home is part of a market which is not under your control.** All we can control is how much risk we put into owning it:

how much we borrow, at what interest rate, how long we live there, how much money we put into it.

- **Your home has more value than as a market investment.** It has returns in terms of security, stability, a legacy, and a roof over your head, not to mention the possibly negative personal costs such as bad memories or a tie to a soon-to-be ex-spouse. But what may be immeasurable is the value of the fact you live in it.

THE REAL COST OF OWNING A HOME

Hands down, the initial outlay of money you need to buy a home these days (and we're not talking about no-money-down mortgages) is a much bigger cost than the security deposit, first/last month's rent, and possible broker fee you need to come up with to rent a home. Here's a quick run-through of the things you'll pay for when you initially purchase a home as well as regular monthly costs (marked with an asterisk):

- Down payment
- Closing costs (8 to 10 percent or more of purchase price, may include some of the items listed below)
- Points or loan origination fees
- Escrow fees
- Title insurance
- Legal fees
- Potential private mortgage insurance (PMI)
- Appraisal fees
- Document prep fees

- Tax service fees
- Credit reporting, credit score fees
- Notary
- Property taxes*
- Homeowner's insurance*
- Maintenance fees* (if condo or co-op)
- Repair and maintenance costs* (such as landscaping and upgrades)

The Real Deal: Framing

How something is worded has a big influence on how you perceive the choices you have. If someone asked you if you were interested in a home equity line of credit (HELOC) that would let you remodel your kitchen, you may feel differently from being asked if you were interested in taking on a second mortgage: borrowing against your home, gambling on your interest rate for the loan (since it's a variable rate), reducing your net worth (because you're turning equity—value—into debt), and paying contractors to run you out for two months. Get my drift? Be aware of how words can be used to alter your perception of reality; listen, but listen for what's real.

Here are a few ways the concepts of mortgage and equity can be framed, depending on your perceptions:

Mortgage = investment
Mortgage = debt
Equity = my personal bank
Equity = net worth

Had you bought at a lull in the housing market and sold at its height in 2007, there is little doubt that all these costs would have been more than worth it; plus, you would also have the value of having a roof over your head. But man, oh man, do these costs add up when you make a few wrong decisions, some under your control and some not. And the best way to keep costs under control is to know what all these costs really are and how much control you have over them, including and outside of that list.

Risk 1

For potential and current homeowners risk is everywhere, like crabgrass on a badly kept lawn. Let's take a look at one of the biggest risks, and costs, that come with buying a home: your **mortgage**. Mortgages used to be a very straightforward cost and involve limited risk. Your options were either a thirty- or a fifteen-year mortgage with a fixed interest rate and a 20 percent down payment. It also used to be that mortgages were much more expensive; at one point in the 1980s, if you had great credit the best interest rate you could get was around 16 percent! And the risk and long-term costs vs. benefits of buying a home always rested on a couple of factors: How long did you plan to live there in order to gain as much value/equity as possible? Did you, and could you, make your mortgage payments on time so you could keep your credit and home in good standing? There was much less risk in terms of losing a ton of money in equity because home values rarely fluctuated more than 5 percent over the decades before 1990. And you were set to gain an average of 3 to 5 percent in return on your money year after year, as long as you stayed in the home five to seven years.

But then along came not only lower interest rates but *funky mort-*

gages, as I like to call them: adjustable-rate mortgages (ARMs) and interest-only mortgages. Both do as they are named: ARMs start at a set low interest rate that adjusts after an agreed-on number of years (three years means you have a 3/1 ARM, five years, a 5/1, and so on) according to a predetermined indicator, such as the London Interbank Offered Rate (LIBOR; an interest rate based on the rate at which banks are lending to each other). Interest-only mortgages look cheap at the outset; you pay only the interest on the loan amount for the first several years, no principal. But these are very costly in the long run. The risk is in your gambling that interest rates will either stay low or fall, while the bank is looking/hoping for you to pay a higher rate. ARMs and interest-onlys put the risk of both *housing market moves* and *interest-rate moves* on you, the homeowner. That's why they're so cheap at first. The lender gives you a discount for the privilege of unshouldering them with a tad of the burden of market risk and interest-rate risk. There is one more risk that you take with a mortgage that adjusts over time: *your income*. ARMs became exploding ARMs during the recession when millions of Americans found their 3/1 or 5/1 ARMs resetting at a time when the recession had taken their jobs, business, and income. Even my husband, when we first bought our home in 2005, was slightly tempted by a 5/1 ARM; fortunately, he's married to me so that was *not* going to happen.

Between the risk of interest rates going up, the housing market going down again (will you be able to sell if you have to?), and whether your income can sustain a huge leap in mortgage payments (or if you'll have a job at all), ARMs and interest-only mortgages are rarely worthwhile. The initial math says, "Wow! I can get more house and have more money freed up every month for three or five or seven years." What the long-term math says is, "Wow. I don't know for sure if I'll be making more money in three or five or seven years, and I don't know if I'll be able to sell before the interest rate resets to something I may not be able to afford." A home should be a long-term investment. **Side with the long-term math.** Unless you're a millionaire who can afford ballooning payments down the road, stick to a thirty- or fifteen-year fixed-rate mortgage, especially these days. As I write, we're still looking at historically low interest rates of below 6 percent—a bargain!

Plus let's just do the math, keeping in mind that all initial discounts in borrowing leave you paying less every month but paying more in the end. Take an interest-only mortgage of $300,000 at 5.8 percent (you get a higher rate because it's interest-only) where you pay interest-only for five years. Your mortgage bill will nearly double after those five years (again, banking on income going up or the ability to refinance), and you'll pay a total of around $350,000 interest on the loan (*more* than the loan itself!). What if you instead went for a fixed-rate thirty-year mortgage at 5 percent? You'd have the same mortgage payment due every month, and you'd pay only around $280,000 in interest. That's a savings not only of the panic attacks you'll have at year 4.5 when you realize you can't pay your new ballooning mortgage, but $70,000 in interest.

Risk 2

Another risk that can cost you in lost return is your **down payment**. Your down payment not only can determine what kind of interest rate you get (along with your credit history) but how much of the house you end up owning compared to the bank, and that can make the difference of being able to sell or not. For example, let's say in

2007 you bought a home with a no-money-down mortgage. So, the home is 100 percent owned by the bank, until you live there long enough to start paying off the principal or until the value of the home goes up beyond the amount of the outstanding mortgage. The reason so many folks took out no-money-down mortgages in the 2000s is because the housing boom was going strong for so many years the thought of a housing market falling was a long-ago-and-faraway possibility. Reality news flash: The housing market can lose—a lot. In markets like Nevada, California, and Florida, homes lost 50 percent or more of their value in a little over a year. That's the extreme, but even if the market lost 5 or 10 percent, if you didn't put any money down, you headed underwater.

Why is being underwater on your mortgage such an important thing to avoid? It means that you're losing money in an investment, you won't be able to borrow against any equity in case of an emergency, and you won't be able to move unless you short sell because you owe the bank more than your home is worth. You can much more easily sell a losing stock at a loss than sell a house that you not only have lost money in but that you don't have a dime invested in. How long do you think it will take for the folks who bought at the peak of the market boom and lost 50 percent of the value of their homes to regain that equity? If the housing market barely budged before the housing bubble, maybe 3 to 5 percent a year for thirty years, it would take more than a decade

What Influences the Value of Your Home?

- Overall economy.
- National and local unemployment.
- National and local materials/construction costs.
- National and local fuel costs.
- Your neighbors, town, and municipality.
- Your school district.
- Demographic changes.
- Care and upkeep.

or two for those homeowners to get any of their equity back. We can't count on 20 percent growth in a year happening again in our lifetime.

This brings us back to Michael's $400,000. Many of us were raised by post-Depression generations who felt that owning your own home was the be-all and end-all of the American Dream and, since homes usually stayed fairly stable in value and came with high interest rates, putting down a big down payment and paying your mortgage off quickly was a good idea. You saved money in interest payments and putting your money in your home was as safe as putting it in a bank—heck, maybe safer. But a better use of Michael's money in today's possibly permanently volatile economy would have been to put down 20 percent so he could lock in that great 5.5 percent rate (at the time) and then pay his mortgage bill every month, on time—no more, no less. When you buy your home, the reality is that both you and your lender are placing bets on how the housing market will perform and how long you'll stay there. Michael should have waited until closer to retirement, after owning for at least five to seven years, before placing such a large bet on his home.

But why exactly should he have put 20 percent down? Lenders have traditionally required 20 percent as a hedge against exactly what happened with the housing bubble—the possibility that the value of your home could fall. It also serves as a way for you to feel vested in your home; it means you have skin in the game. If you didn't put any money down, how much would you feel you really own your home compared to someone who saved up for years to put down 20 percent? A *solid down payment* is a good actuarial hedge for the lender, but it also *protects you* from being unable to sell your home. Why? Think of it as a 20 percent protection pillow; if the value of your home drops after you buy, you'd still own some of your home (have equity), as long as the market didn't drop more than 20 percent. Granted, for many of us, depending on when you bought, that may have happened. But a 20 percent cushion is bigger than a 10 percent cushion; you can come back from a 30 percent drop in home value faster if the spread—what you owe vs. what it's worth—is smaller. And as we've seen, it's incredibly difficult to sell your home when you owe more than you're going to get at sale time. So why not put down 30 percent or more so you never have to worry about being able to sell? Because that's too much of a bet that the market will fall that far, and it may not be the most efficient use of your money. Put down too much, and not only can you still get stuck in your home, owing more than it's worth, but you've got too much skin in the game. Too much to lose.

What about when it comes time to move? I heard from hundreds of folks in 2009 who had lost their jobs and had an ARM explode; because they didn't put much money down on their home, they were unable to sell. Their beloved homes had become anchors. Because when it comes time to sell, that fantasy equity becomes very, very real. Lenders don't want to lose money either. Say your mortgage is $380,000 but your home is now only worth $300,000. No lender really wants to sell a home with negative equity, especially at an $80,000 loss. Times have changed a bit with all the potential foreclosures just waiting to happen, and many lenders are accepting short sales (when you sell your home for less than the outstanding mortgage) if you can find a buyer, but they'd rather not take the hit. Of the four million foreclosures on the market in 2009, you can bet that many were underwater, and the homeowner was unable to short sell.

It can seem like making a down payment and paying down your principal can be a matter of chasing your home value when the market tanks. And sometimes, in a drastic housing bubble, it makes sense to think about how worthwhile it is to continue to put money into something that has lost 50 percent of its value (more on walking away soon). But in general, looking historically and taking the recent housing market drama into account, it makes a lot of sense to try to limit your risk of owning a home by putting down 20 percent. A 20 percent down payment also lowers costs in other ways:

- **Lower fixed interest rates.** Lenders reserve their lowest interest rates for those not only with great credit, but for those who put down 20 percent or more.
- **Lower risk of being underwater.** The chances of a housing market drop of another 20 percent within a year or two is again slim. But another 5 percent or so? Totally possible. You want to try to limit the chances of being unable to sell because you're underwater. If you put down 20 percent and the market drops 7 percent, you're in the clear. For example, if you put down $40,000 (20 percent) on a home with a sale price and value of $200,000 and the value drops $15,000, you still own part of your home. But if you only put down $10,000 (5 percent) and the value drops $15,000, you're underwater.
- **Lower interest payments.** Lower interest rates translate into lower interest payments and lower monthly mortgage payments over the life of the loan. Voilà!

All that being said, did I put 20 percent down on my home? Nope. But hypocrite I am not; slight risk-taker I am. At the time my husband and I bought in 2005, we had enough saved for a 10 percent cash down payment on an apartment in New York City. (If you know anything about the city, you know that it's ridiculously pricey to own a home.) We got a thirty-year fixed-rate mortgage and bought a bit less house than we could afford—no matter how much the hubby wanted to spend more. We both understood that by putting down only 10 percent and piggybacking (attaching another loan) a home equity line of credit (HELOC) for the other 10 percent so we could qualify for the 20 percent down payment rate, we had to make a commitment to stay put. No moving or selling for at least five years because we owned only 10 percent of our home while the bank owned the other 90 percent. Not a lot of wiggle room should the market decide to dive the year or two or three after we moved in. So, we've lived here six years now and we've seen our value go up 40 percent at the height of the market and then drop about 15 percent by 2010 for a current net value increase of 25 percent, less than 5 percent a year. Had we bought at the height of the market with only 10 percent down, we'd have to stay put at least *another* five years or more to keep our heads above water. If we had put down 20 percent at the height of the market, we'd almost break even today. Of course, we'd never have been able to afford to buy at the height! Putting less than 20 percent down is always a risk, and we respected that risk. We also bought a small enough house that we could afford our mortgage on little more than one salary, if need be. But I don't recommend putting down less than 10 percent, especially considering the shakiness of the housing market in the past couple of years.

Unfortunately, not only did millions of people use no-money-down mortgages over the past ten years, but the government is behind a lot of low-money-down mortgages, also known as Federal Housing Administration (FHA) loans. FHA loans used to be much more benign when the housing market fluctuated no more than

5 percent a year. But a program that lets you put only 3.5 percent down is scary. I've seen too many people trapped in their homes, with ruined credit because they couldn't make their mortgage payments and also couldn't sell because they were underwater more than 4 percent—much more.

Yes, putting together a down payment for a home on a modest salary can be very hard. But I'd be irresponsible to recommend bypassing that pain to get something you want. Surely, it's difficult to say no to low down payments especially when the FHA makes it so hard to say no. In 2010, they announced a plan to allow the first-time home buyer's tax credit (max of $8,000) to be applied directly to closing costs and down payments on a 3.4 percent mortgage. If the mortgage was small enough, that could result in you putting 0 percent down out of pocket. Resist.

Here's when putting down less than 10 percent is okay: when you have family who can swoop in to the rescue and make your mortgage payments should you lose your job or income. If you can't save up another 7 percent to make it a clean 10 percent in the next five years, the home is probably too much for your checkbook.

Risk 3

Managing your mortgage can sometimes be like managing any other investment. Make enough of a return (in home-speak, that would be *equity*), and you can borrow against it. I'm referring to **HELOCs and home equity loans**. These loans are no longer the piggy banks they came to be before the credit crisis, but they're still out there, and they still carry risk. The new rule is that lenders won't even consider lending you money off of your equity until you're at least 30 percent above water, meaning you owe 70 percent or less of the home's value. It used to be that if you had even just 10 percent equity, you could borrow against your home (as my husband and I did). That practice is gone. Also gone, we hope, is the attitude that our homes are piggy banks so why not just tap into them when we want.

Remember, until you pay off your mortgage, or at a minimum pay off 50 percent of it, the majority of your home belongs to your lender, and to the market. So, let's say you have 40 percent equity in your home and you'd like to take 20 percent out with a HELOC to update your kitchen and bath. You'll have the additional cost of a monthly HELOC payment, plus the gap between the return on your remodeling (when you sell) and the loan, which runs about 20 percent. However, as I can attest to personally, the costs may be worth it: You won't have to take another bath in a thirty-year-old tub or cook in a grimy kitchen. But there's one risk that few take fully into account: *HELOCs have variable interest rates.* Let's say you get a HELOC for $20,000 at the going rate (as I write) of 3 percent. Your monthly payments would be $50. But if your rate jumps to 8 percent, you're looking at a monthly bill of $133+. Make sure you can swing it.

> One benefit of HELOCs and home equity loans: The interest you pay is a tax deduction. Sweet!

And be honest with yourself. *HELOCs and home equity loans are like second and third mortgages.* They turn your equity into debt. This used to be a desperate and shameful thing. I remember my father, laid off after the Black October crash in the late 1980s, sitting the whole family (of eight) down at the kitchen table to tell us the very distressing news that he was going to have to take out a second mortgage on the house to help pay the bills. He was very distressed at having to turn hard-earned equity (we'd lived there for over ten years) into debt.

Alert

Don't take equity out of your home to pay off credit card debt (with a HELOC, home equity loan, or refinancing).

You may get a lower rate but you've now tied up your debt in your house. If you can't pay your credit card bill, they will not come take your house. If you can't pay your mortgages, they *will* take your house.

Keep plastic debt plastic. Protect your home.

Refinancing is another initial benefit with long-term risk and cost. Your monthly payments may be smaller, but you'll pay more in interest over time—think of it as stretching your mortgage out, eating up your investment earnings. Let's say you have a $300,000 mortgage right now at 6 percent and you qualify for a new rate of 5 percent, but you've already been paying your mortgage for five years so you only have twenty-five years to go (always keep that in mind). If you "refi" into another thirty-year mortgage at 5 percent, you'll save around $350 a month but you'll save less than $100 in interest payments over the life of the loan. The interest savings of 1 percent is wiped out by stretching the mortgage out over the five years you've already paid. The best way to garner true savings when you refinance, especially if you plan on staying in your home ten years or more, is to refinance into a better mortgage—one that already reflects some of the years you've put into it, say a fifteen-year mortgage. If you don't plan on

---

Another Risk: Your Neighbors

Research local neighborhood guidelines (such as cutting the grass and clearing the sidewalks of snow), condo/co-op finances, and local foreclosure rates before buying.

---

staying put more than five years, you may reap the monthly savings (and enjoy them!), but watch out for closing costs. Refinancing is like buying your home over again so closing costs can be a huge expense. Roll them into your new mortgage, if your lender allows it and if interest rates are cheap and you're staying put for at least five years to lessen the cost. If you move too soon, the closing costs associated with refinancing will cost you too much.

Risk 4

How much home you buy can determine a lot about your financial future. **Too much house = disaster.** One of the most common questions I get is "How do I know how much home I can afford?" If and when your combined costs for mortgage(s), property taxes, home insurance, and maintenance (if you have a co-op or condo) get above 34 percent of your monthly take-home income, you get into dangerous territory. Keeping housing costs to about a third of your monthly expenses lowers your risks of being unable to afford your home should your income go down; plus it leaves money for all the other demands of life like food, clothes, transportation, saving for retirement, cash savings, and saving for college. During the recent housing bubble too many people bought homes not only too big to maintain but too big for their paychecks. Your eyes shouldn't be bigger than your checkbook. And if you keep your housing costs low, since it is the biggest bite out of your budget pie, you'll have the freedom to do the other things you want and need to do with your money. A too-big house can feel like a prison when your income goes down or fails to go up or a mortgage resets to a higher interest rate. Don't put your future finances or your family's security in jeopardy by thinking you can handle 45 percent housing costs. The closer to 30 percent you are, the less your home will cost you, especially over time.

The Cost of Prepaying Your Mortgage

Our homes are not ephemeral like stocks, which you can't reach out and touch. We live in our homes, build and raise families in them. Owning your home can be all about security, stability, and a feeling of accomplishment (more on the personal costs/benefits of owning a home soon). This is why one of the most common beefs in the money world is about prepaying your mortgage. After the stock market tanked in 2009, many folks decided to put their money into something they can touch and feel, something with utility, the roof over their heads, and tried to pay more than their monthly mortgage payments to pay off their homes sooner. But does it make financial sense to pay more on your mortgage than the lender asks every month? We could ask Michael the $400,000 question, but let's spare him that painful reality and look at where your money is better put.

It's not realistic, first of all, to make a one-to-one comparison of the housing market vs. the stock market. This is because the average homeowner stays in his or her home for five to eight years. Most of us invest in the stock market (usually in our retirement accounts) for a longer time frame, closer to twenty years. The time you sell your investments (your home, for example)—how long you hold vs. when you fold—is a huge factor in determining any gains or losses. The cost of buying and selling our homes quickly doesn't bode well for making money. Like the stock market, we'd need to stay in for at least ten years to guarantee some return, and fifteen to twenty years to get double-digit gains.

Most folks who ask about prepaying a mortgage, especially as a security move, are planning on staying put in their homes for as long as possible or even until retirement. Still, does it make financial sense? *Consumer Reports* ran an excellent scenario (taking into account everything from mutual fund fees to taxes and mortgage deductions) pitting $100 extra paid into a thirty-year fixed-rate mortgage vs. $100 invested in the S&P 500 from 1969 through 2008. They found that if you held on to both for fifteen years or more, the stock market won out every time—by a lot. In a ten-year window, the S&P won out most of the time and the mortgage was ahead only a few times, but not by much.

Another example of how the math doesn't necessarily work out: My good friend and fantastic certified financial planner (CFP) Gregg Fisher, of Gerstein Fisher, ran his company's own mortgage vs. investing scenario. He began to see too many clients hedging their bets with their mortgages in reaction to a tanking stock market and wanted to illustrate the real costs. He ran a few scenarios: a client paying off a mortgage in full and then afterward starting to invest what used to be a mortgage payment into the market, a client who prepaid her mortgage over the years but also maintained an investment portfolio simultaneously, and a client who didn't prepay at all and invested solely in the market. In each scenario, the client who stuck with the stock market only, not prepaying at all, over thirty years came out $1 million ahead—earning 24 percent if there's deflation and 15 percent with inflation.

So why pay your mortgage off early if it loses you money in the end? Because it makes you feel better. There are many folks who are happy to stick to bonds rather than stocks because they'd prefer to feel safer and don't like the volatility of the stock market, even if the odds say they'll make more money over time with stocks. It's the same with your home. You may feel much more secure and solid putting an extra $200 toward your principal and shaving five years off your mortgage so you can retire without having to worry about housing payments. After all, getting rid of a 30 percent piece of your monthly budget will feel great.

Just be aware that there is a price you pay for going with your gut as opposed to the math. The cost of prepaying gets higher the lower the interest rate on your mortgage. It helps to stay put and focus pre-payments only on the home that you'll be retiring in. Prepaying your mortgage, especially when your interest rate is below 10 percent and you're planning on moving in five to ten years, makes almost no sense. What if the housing market goes down again? Down goes your equity and money. That's not a security or stability move—that's a gamble on your home value going up.

OWNING: IS THE COST WORTHWHILE?

It seems un-American to say that owning a home is not for everyone and that it should not necessarily be the be-all and end-all of the American Dream. But that doesn't make it any less true. There are times in your life when it makes sense to own a home and times when it doesn't, and there's nothing to be ashamed or embarrassed about when you rent. I once had a young professional come to me and say that now that she was getting married, her family was bugging her and her fiancé about buying: "After all, renting is like flushing your money down the toilet, right?" Not always and not really. Unless the housing market is booming like crazy, you bought at a low price, and you time your sale at exactly the right month, renting can actually save you money.

The real cost of homeownership can make sense for you if you can answer yes to the following questions:

- Do you plan on staying put for at least five years?
- Do you have a measure of job security?
- Do you have six to eight months of living expenses saved up outside your down payment?
- Do you have at least 10 percent to put down? And if not and you put less down, are you willing and able to stay in the home longer to build some equity?
- Is homeownership important to you both personally and financially, as a way to build net worth and a family legacy?

And what about if you just can't replicate a winning investment portfolio (like the ones mentioned) or you just don't have access to those investments? Maybe the home values in your area continue—or will—go up at a much higher rate than projected? (This happens when there's a great demand for housing due to, say, a new corporation setting up headquarters nearby.) Or you just could get very, very lucky like the residents of hot neighborhoods that saw a dip but can't escape long-term growth because of their location and need for easy-access housing. These are all scenarios in which the costs of owning are mitigated or assuaged.

Sure, there are many people (and finance gurus) who are very vocal about how they've made money in the real estate market, but the factors in the how and why are not easily replicated. Timing of the market and when you buy and sell are rarely mentioned and there's always an assumption that home values go up—that you're getting a deal now.

Risk and the sad stories are rarely mentioned, but I can assure you that I have heard too many. My sister-in-law, who's struggling to keep her home as her commissions and income tanked with the recession. A friend who had a booming real estate business only to see it all disappear with the housing bust, leaving her in near bankruptcy. The well-known television personality who told me that he wanted to foreclose on two investment properties because he was almost 50 percent underwater on both and "there's no help" for people like him.

There will always be people tooting the get-rich-quick-with-real-estate horn. Just as there will always be someone on Wall Street

> **But It's a Buyer's Market!**
>
> Sure, there are great reasons to buy:
>
> • Market is priced low.
> • Tax credits.
> • Low mortgage rates.
> • Tax deductions.
>
> But it's not a buyer's market for you if you can't buy right.

touting the newest, best stock pick. But your primary residence, your home, shouldn't be about getting rich quick. It should be not only an investment of your money but your energy and desire to build a life under that very roof. Owning a home must come with a commitment to realize not only financial gains but personal ones as well. You don't want to own for two or three years only to spend half of that time messing with (and paying for) a bad water heater or a mold problem. But once you commit, like any relationship, it can pay off personally for many years. I've owned the same home with my husband for six years, and though we're looking at a return of maybe 5 percent after the housing bust (if we had sold at the height of the market our return would have been more like 20 percent. D'oh!), we're also looking at a dozen-acre park opening up next year just down the block with full views of Manhattan and the Brooklyn Bridge. We're looking at neighborhood demand going up every year, especially since we're in one of the most coveted school districts and have a cherished spot in the parking lot across the street that comes with our building. We're also most enjoying the fact that we're able to walk our daughter four blocks to school. We've made wonderful friendships with our neighbors, which has paid off in many immeasurable (and measurable in saved baby-sitting money!) ways. Sure, we could possibly feel the same if we rented but we do feel more fully vested not only in our building but in our community because we own part of it. Sometimes that's a good thing, sometimes it's not. Decide what you value in terms of your lifestyle as well as your means.

In the end, some basic rules apply that can help assuage the cost of owning a home: Don't buy too much house—go smaller than you think. Don't plan on moving for at least five to seven years. Lock in a fixed-rate mortgage. Do your neighborhood research. Insist on a home inspection. Be realistic about the hidden costs. And most important, find the joy in owning the roof over your head. It's there, and it helps lower the costs.

Real $$$ Cost of Owning a Home	Real Personal Cost of Owning a Home
Extensive cash savings for down payment, or risky loan to replace cash savings	Inability to move quickly into another home
Long and large debt obligation/contract	Time loss and physical strain of maintenance and repairs
Property taxes	Distress due to unexpected maintenance/repairs
Maintenance (possibly fluctuating greatly)	Risk to quality of life due to financial constraints
Lost income hours due to maintenance	Personal burden of hefty financial responsibilities
Short term: possible drastic changes in value/return	
Long term: possible low rate of return	
Effect costs, such as longer, more expensive commute	

Real $$$ Benefits of Owning a Home	Real Personal Benefits of Owning a Home
Possible solid returns on investment	Shelter
Possible tax deductions	Sense of security/stability
Hedge against more risky investments over the long term	Sense of community

Real $$$ Benefits of Owning a Home	Real Personal Benefits of Owning a Home
Can build net worth/wealth	Symbol of success
	Freedom to alter the space with construction/remodeling to suit changing needs/likes
	Place to build memories, history, forge identity

RENTING

But what if you don't have any qualms about renting, even if you have the money to own? Maybe you move every couple of years and need to be mobile because of your job or career. Maybe you don't need to own a home to fulfill any personal need or desire and you see home-ownership as a financial transaction, no more, no less. The American Dream to you may be about something different—freedom to work in a field you enjoy or just plain prosperity, which to you is more about your bank balance than brick. I've also met many folks who just don't want all the financial and personal costs of being a homeowner—the headaches that happen when the broiler breaks, dealing with plumbers and contractors, having to unclog your own toilet and pay for the garbage pickup. And there are others who are convinced that the stock market holds more gains for them (and historically it has) than the housing market in the area they live, so they'd rather put their money there than into the ground.

In many cases right now across the country, it makes a lot more financial sense to rent than to buy, though my goal isn't to scare you into renting forever. But more of you should be renting than are currently renting. Why? Because just as not everyone can or should eat nuts, not everyone can or should own a home. Before teasing out just when it makes sense to rent vs. buy, here are the obvious costs of renting:

- Finder fee to real estate agent.
- Monthly rent.
- One month's security deposit plus possibly last month's rent.
- Renter's insurance.

Not so complicated and, in many places, not as expensive as owning. You get the same school district, same municipal resources, a roof, and so on, without the hassle of mortgages, property taxes, and maintenance. However, you may miss out on benefiting from a healthy real estate market. For example, if my husband and I had decided to sell our home at the height of the real estate bubble, in 2008, we would have $100,000 more cash in our pocket now. But we plan on staying put for a long time. There's still a big chance that we will recoup that $100,000 in the next five years. Based on how much we put down and into the mortgage, that's a better performance than our other investments. But what if it isn't, and when does it cost less to rent and instead put your money somewhere else?

There's a good old-fashioned rule I like: **The Rule of 15**.

- Take the monthly rent of the place you're interested in and multiply by 12 to calculate how much the rent would cost you in a year. (Say, $1,500 a month would mean $18,000 a year.)
- Multiply your annual rent by 15. (In this case, $18,000 × 15 = $270,000.)

- Compare that amount to the going asking price of a comparable home for sale in the same area.

If the sale price of a comparable home is much higher than your annual rent times 15, the market still has a way down to go. If your annual rent times 15 is higher than a comparable sale price, then you've got yourself a buyer's market. But again, you have to be in a good place to buy.

Real $$$ Cost of Renting	Real Personal Cost of Renting
Possible loss of potential long-term gains from owning	Inability to change/alter surroundings substantially
Rents can be higher than mortgages for same space/area	At mercy of landlord contract/relationship
Risk of owner breaking contract/foreclosing, resulting in sudden search for and move into new home	Possible effect on sense of place and community, even accomplishment

Real $$$ Benefits of Renting	Real Personal Benefits of Renting
Ability to move easily (within confines of lease and/or agreement of landlord) and cheaply	Able to move more freely than homeowner
Lower initial costs than down payment for homeowner	Not responsible for stress and time related to maintenance
Little or no maintenance costs	
Lower rents (than mortgages) free up funds for other investments/plans	

THE REAL COST OF GETTING IN TROUBLE WITH YOUR HOME

Had I written this book three years ago, the chances of the following pages existing as more than just a couple of paragraphs would be slim. Before the burst of the housing bubble, few of us knew what a loan modification entailed or what a short sale was, and few would even consider something as drastic as walking away. We live in a new reality that unfortunately has made these scenarios all too real for millions of us. And for the rest of us who say "This can't happen to me," it's always good to be prepared.

First, the Mortgage

The federal government's Making Home Affordable Program turned the term *loan modification* into common knowledge. Loan modifications do exactly what they sound like—the lender changes the terms of your loan. Why a loan modification rather than refinance? Because to refinance, you need proof of income, great credit, and money for closing costs, three things that usually are not present when someone is in enough trouble to ask for a modification. Loan modifications are reserved for folks who cannot manage their mortgage payments but have just enough to maybe squeak by if one or two hundred dollars were shaved off every month. So what does a loan mod do? It should reduce your principal; after all, when your home is now worth $180,000 and your mortgage is $300,000, there's little that shaving a point of interest is going to do to lessen your load. A loan modification usually has the lender reduce your interest rate, but you still owe the full amount of the outstanding mortgage, no matter what the value of your home is now. What's the cost of a loan modification? Usually an extended mortgage, term with fees and lost interest tacked on the end, making a seventeen-year mortgage turn into a thirty, for example. Thankfully, Washington pressured for change when it comes to your credit score and reports. In the past, a loan modification would get you just as bad a credit score as someone who just dropped off the keys and ran. Now, loan modifications are to be categorized as a different type of change to your loan so the credit damage isn't as high—but it's still there. What are the possibilities of getting a loan modification? Very slim. In 2009, of the millions of applications for the Making Home Affordable Program, only 3 percent were given full loan modifications.

Leaving Home

If you're just unable to make your mortgage payments, no matter how low they could go, do what you can to either rent your home out for a profit or to break even or sell as soon as possible (this means investing in a fantastic local real estate agent, grassroots marketing, and elbow grease). But you can sell in the regular way only if you have equity in your home. The sale price must be more than your outstanding mortgage, or mortgages if you have more than one. If it's too close or much below, you have to try for a **short sale**. With more than 30 percent of American homeowners underwater as I write, and up to 48 percent of us underwater by 2011, short sales, once a rather clandestine bank policy, are much more common. A short sale usually requires you to get a buyer, agree on a price, then present both the buyer (and his or her credit) and the price to your lender. Your lender must accept the offer and the buyer before you can sell. Why would a lender agree to trading one mortgage for a smaller mortgage on the same home? Because it may cost the bank less than letting your home foreclose.

What's the cost to you of a short sale? It used to be that the difference between the mortgages was considered forgiven debt by the IRS, and you'd have to pay taxes on it. For example, if you owe the bank $300,000, but you short sell at $250,000, you would have had to pay taxes on the $50,000 of the loan that was forgiven. We can be thankful that's out the window. (If you can't manage a mortgage payment, how could you manage taxes on five or six figures worth of debt?) The Mortgage Debt Forgiveness Relief Act of 2007 got rid of that practice. Now, if you short sell, you are not only forgiven the debt owed but also the taxes on that debt. But your credit will pay. Anytime you change the terms of a loan—especially one as big as a mortgage—your credit goes up or down, depending on if you made a better or worse deal. A short sale will damage your credit on par with a foreclosure.

So why short sell? Why not foreclose?

Foreclosure comes with its own messy costs. Not only will your credit score suffer enough to keep you from borrowing at any decent rate for three to seven years, but you'll endure months of stressful encounters with your lender. (Though not your taxman; remember, as long as it's your primary residence, you will not be held accountable to paying taxes on what you owe.) Also, once foreclosure notices are sent, you must be aware that your friendly neighborhood sheriff could arrive on your doorstep to physically kick you out.

The psychological cost of foreclosure is one of the biggest costs in our financial *and* personal lives. Foreclosure, which is basically losing your home not of your will, is a tremendously stressful experience. Before foreclosure, you live day in and day out with the threat of losing your home. Having your home taken away from you is akin to having your place identity stripped, a sudden loss of community, the devastation of possibly lifelong dreams. Who wants to lose his or her home? No one. And recovery from foreclosure is a long, hard uphill battle that includes mourning your loss and garnering back the confidence to get back to where you once were. But financially, you'd be surprised at how quickly you can recover. Because, although the foreclosure will remain on your credit reports for seven to ten years, you will be able to get another mortgage in around three years, though you must ask yourself if jumping back in the real estate pool at that point is a wise decision. At least you know that your credit score will go up enough—as long as everything else remains in good standing—much sooner than seven to ten years. Foreclosure is not a death sentence. It's temporary.

And what if you actually want to foreclose? Is **walking away** ever a good idea? Foreclosing brings down the value of your neighbors' homes and means that you've reneged on a contract you signed, but at what point are the financial and personal costs of foreclosing outweighed by the long-term cost of staying put? It's estimated that in the last quarter of 2009, a measly 35 percent of foreclosures were by folks who had the money to pay their mortgage but just decided that it wasn't worth paying anymore—these are called *strategic defaults* or walking away. Let's say you live in California in a city (like Modesto) where over 80 percent of homes are worth less than their mortgages and 25 percent of those are underwater by more than 25 percent. Some great research from the University of Arizona by Brent T. White in December 2009 looked at the folks who walked away from their mortgages or chose not to. Professor White's conclusion? "The real mystery is not why large numbers of homeowners are walking away, but why, given the percentage of underwater mortgages, more homeowners are not."

Foreclosure FYI

If you know that you may have to foreclose or you're planning to foreclose, make sure that you work to **secure another place to live (a rental) before your credit takes the foreclosure hit**. You have some control over just how much foreclosure will cost your quality of life if you directly face the possibility of it happening and plan as much as you can beforehand.

This paper was met with horror by many in the media, government officials, and bankers alike, but turn the question around and ask, Why should someone lose potentially six figures paying the mortgage on a money pit that may not regain its value for fifteen to twenty years, when lenders so easily walked away from their responsibilities to us, the borrowers, with funky loans and credit default swaps, creating a housing bubble that burst, leaving many regular Americans with gum on their face? (And little to show for it but negative equity.) If your home is now worth $160,000 and your mortgage is $300,000, how long do you stay? Obviously you don't stay because you think the home is a great investment.

I was giving a talk recently to a group of very accomplished women with ample investments. At the cocktail party beforehand, a successful retiree took me aside to chat and told me about the mess her daughter and her husband are in in Arizona. They had bought a home in 2007 for over $300,000 with a mortgage of $300,000 at the time. Homes on her street were now (summer of 2010) selling for around $80,000. The husband was adamant that they should honor their contract and stay put; after all, the market would go back up, right? This retiree, the mom, had been nudging them to walk away; savvy investor and former employee of a big bank, this grande dame was all about the Benjamins. She asked me, "If they stay put, how long will it take to recoup their money?" Analysts are saying it will take fifteen to twenty years in that part of the country, if they're lucky. Madame Retiree took that as me saying that I agreed that they should walk away. But as I didn't know their full financial situation, I followed up with, "Just tell them to keep in mind the rest of their finances and their future plans. How much is that home worth to them personally? Do they love it? Are they happy and proud of it? Or is there a chance that your daughter will get to a point where she's had enough and they're willing to endure the possible consequences of ruined credit, for example?"

According to a study by the National Bureau of Economic Research, 81 percent of homeowners said it was immoral to default on a mortgage. The study also found that once a home was more than 10 percent underwater, "moral and social considerations" were the "most important variables predicting strategic default." Is shame and social stigma worth possibly losing $1,000 or more a month for at least twenty years? Economists have a nice derogatory name for the 81 percent of Americans who don't make rational financial decisions: *woodheads*. As we know, more than many economists did before the advent of behavioral economics, we are not always rational creatures.

Fear of walking away is more justified in some states than others. In some states (called *recourse states*), if you choose to walk away from your home, a lender can come after your other assets, even garnish your wages—this is called a *deficiency judgment*. However, the chances of such a judgment happening are very slim in a market overwhelmed with foreclosures. But other states are nonrecourse states. In these states you actually pay a surcharge on your mortgage (at closing) because the lender has little power over you besides the collateral of the home. If you walk away, the lender cannot come after your other assets.

So, what's the cost of walking away? Ruined credit, various psychological and possibly social consequences (depends on if you're happy to walk or are devastated), damage to your neighborhood's property value, and adding to the foreclosure burden on the economy. However, facing years, possibly decades, of being tied to a devalued investment that may begin to serve little personal good as well (what is a financial burden may turn into a huge psychological burden as time passes) may be too high a cost for you to handle.

Real $$$ Cost of Losing a Home to Foreclosure or Walking Away	Real Personal Cost of Losing a Home to Foreclosure or Walking Away
Devastated credit record/scores	Feeling of failure
Inability to borrow at competitive rates for three to seven years	Distress of foreclosure/bank/legal proceedings
Possible legal repercussions (depending on state)	Distress over relocation
Possible government or bank repercussions (taxes)	Family/loved ones affected by loss/move
Contributing to lower home values of neighbors and national foreclosure burden	Social stigma
Possible effect on job search if credit is reviewed before hiring	Guilt over neighborhood repercussions and/or breaking contract

Real $$$ Benefits of Losing a Home to Foreclosure or Walking Away	Real Personal Benefits of Losing a Home to Foreclosure or Walking Away
Frees up finances for other needs	Lessens stress of maintaining a possibly unmanageable financial obligation or stress of a deeply negative return on what's perceived to be a personal/financial benefit
Frees up finances to invest in possible better return	Freedom and ability to start over
Ability to rebuild credit and borrow and/or own again in two to three years	

The Real Cost of
Marriage and Divorce

*A stressful marriage can be as bad for
the heart as a regular smoking habit.*

—*The New York Times Magazine,* April 18, 2010

We're not getting married so much anymore. At least, some of
us are not.

Of all thirty- to forty-four-year-olds in this country, only 60 percent were married in 2007. The Pew Research Center says that, back
in the day (circa 1970), 84 percent of us were married—a mighty
drop-off in less than forty years from a norm of thousands of years.
Granted, some of us can't get married by law (yet), but of those
who can, what's keeping us from what's been touted as the best social
construct since Eden? There's a perception that getting married
and getting divorced just costs too much, not only in money but in
effort, commitment, time, family drama, and so on. Much of the research pertaining to marriage comes at it from either a pro-marriage
angle or pro-singles or pro-cohabitation. Wherever the research
comes from, the general bias is that getting married is a costly wager

(including the possible pricey result of divorce). In light of that monster price tag, let's start with the benefits, how marriage pays off personally and financially.

I'm on my second marriage. Really.

I had what's fittingly called in my case a starter marriage, a brief but transformative bad judgment in my twenties. I learned a lot. Mostly that the older you are, the better your judgment!

So, I married again in my thirties, happily and now long. Why did I do it? If that first d'oh! cost me so much financially and personally, why take the risk of doing it again when some folks would argue that just living together costs so much less? Because I respect the commitment that it is and wanted that commitment. Because I wanted to bring a child into a married household where both parents are invested in his or her care and well-being, personally and legally. Because I want no hospital or judge to make decisions for me instead of my life partner or to deny my partner any rights. Because maybe I'm a bit old-fashioned and buy into the idea of a long married life together and all that it entails.

But that's me. Why does everyone else get married if it costs so darn much, financially and personally, especially if it doesn't work out? Commitment is one answer. The idea that someone is pledging themselves to take care of you ("in sickness and in health"), to grow old with you, to maybe grow and raise a family with you is a powerful one. We have a primal need to mate. There's much argument over the idea of whether we're wired to mate for life like gibbons and turtledoves or if we (especially men) are wired to mate multiple times. We can all agree that many if not most human beings have a desire for connection. The commitment that a marriage is and what it symbolizes says to everyone, We two are making a pledge to stick together through thick and thin, to care for each other, until death do us part. Now, whether that actually happens, the idea that you are not going it alone, that someone will be there for you, can be priceless.

Pressure and expectations from the outside can also push us toward marriage. Religion and tradition play a huge part in marriage plans. Why else would some parents practically bankrupt themselves to throw a party? Sponsoring a large wedding for your kids is one way of both fulfilling family and cultural expectations as well as signifying to others that you are successful and able to support such a party. It can seem like an old-fashioned and expensive tradition, but it's difficult to undo centuries of dowries and arranged marriages with only a couple of decades of change. And the ideas and dreams some have of their wedding day can well outstrip an actual budget. However, the pressure to present a certain image, throw a certain party, invite cousins you haven't seen since you were three years old, or fulfill a childhood dream of being a princess-for-a-day cannot be underestimated or swept aside. After all, it's an over $50 billion industry, not even counting indirect sales, and surely many of us don't have that money to spend.

Being married means the possibility of living cheaper and becoming more financially stable over time. Two incomes (the majority of married couples these days both work) means two ways to pay the bills. Of course, in the recession, many married couples saw little or no stability—it's not a super-shield from getting laid off—but imagine if each partner had been going through the same hard times solo. If you both work, instead of trying to maintain a household by yourself on one salary, with an expensive benefits plan and expensive childcare costs, you have an economic partner not only in taking on all budget items and benefits but in getting better benefits from employers, a perk that unmarried cohabiters are not privy to.

Why else would a whole segment of society be fighting for the right to marry if it were really nothing but paper? It may be paper, but it's powerful paper. It gives you the right to property and assets should your spouse pass away before you. It gives you rights to your children you may not have if not a spouse. It gives you the legal ability to visit the hospital and make medical decisions should your partner be unable to. You have the right, over other family, to make burial decisions and plans. You file joint taxes and possibly (depending on your tax bracket) pay less. You can escape estate and gift taxes when one of you passes away. You receive Social Security, Medicare, and disability benefits for a spouse. Employers must take you on, should you elect, to receive benefits.

One of the first questions an employer and/or insurer asks when you enroll in a benefits plan is if you are married or single. If you live together but aren't married, you would each pay a separate, higher cost for your health insurance, life insurance, and retirement benefits. Let's say $150 is taken out of each of your paychecks a month for *health coverage*. But if you were married and covered under the same plan, the cost would be closer to $220 for you two, rather than $300 for you in total as singles. Here are more areas in which a policy or coverage plan for married couples costs less than two individual plans/policies:

- **Auto insurance plans.** For some plans, what matters is that you're combining two policies into one or now sharing cars; for others it's about less risky behavior because you're married. Either way, you're looking at discounts of 10 to 50 percent, depending on your policyholder. The biggest discounts of 25 to 50 percent are for young couples; their rates are higher due to their ages and subsequent higher risk pool.

- **Home insurance.** Some insurers give small but meaningful discounts on home insurance policies and rental policies if you're married—for example, $5 off a month.
- **Basic banking.** When my husband and I linked our accounts and opened a joint account, we got more than $20 a month in fees waived, though some banks do this for couples who are not married as well.
- **Credit card rates and plans.** If you have a joint card, and your spouse has better credit than you, you will now enjoy the discount in your interest rate due to having a better combined rate. Some card issuers will offer you discounts for adding a family member as an authorized user on the account.
- **Life insurance policies.** Actuaries count on the odds that if you're married, you'll adopt a healthier lifestyle—though much research shows that, on average, married couples gain ten or more pounds each in the first five years of marriage. Also, studies show that married men tend to live longer.
- **Gym memberships.** Couples and families get discounts for signing up a spouse and/or child. Many gyms don't care if a couple is married or not, but many also limit their best deals to family members and spouses only.
- **Mortgage costs.** Especially if one of you has a much better credit score than the other and you go in together on the mortgage.
- **Taxes.** This applies to the around 50 percent of married couples who have a big income disparity. In this case, annual tax savings

filing jointly as a married couple can be over $1,000. Conversely, married couples who make similar incomes can suffer the marriage penalty, paying more.

- **Spending.** Couples and families get discounts for many things, even restaurant specials and neighborhood store promotions. It's about the business or benefit of getting two for one; hence businesses can charge less since one customer is now automatically two.

But also consider the fact that you have someone to help you pay the bills, period. Marriage is a tribal pooling of resources, not only financially but for childcare and our modern version of hunting and gathering—grocery shopping and errands.

Most women work now (especially during and after the recent Great Recession, aka the Mancession, where 75 percent or more of the jobs lost were held by men) and one-third of married women make more than their husbands, a number that gets close to half when you include those making more than $55,000. Women are also more highly educated these days than ever, bringing even more economic stability (and hireability) to the table. The stats say that married adults continue to see larger gains in household income than unmarried adults. Married couples have seen their income go up almost 60 percent since the 1980s, while overall households looked at only 44 percent gains.

The greatest gains in terms of the likelihood of getting (and staying) married are for those with a college education. Almost forty years ago, the chances of getting married were nearly the same between those with lower education levels and those with higher education. Not anymore. The Pew Research Center found that in 2007, only

43 percent of women and 45 percent of men without a high school education were married, whereas 69 percent of both men and women with a college degree were married. Marriage is becoming a way of life that seems to go along with a college diploma. Also, like tends to marry like these days. If you've got a degree, you're more likely to marry someone who has a similar education level, and so on.

Of course, marriage and kids don't necessarily go hand in hand, but they seem to when it comes to being well off. Harvard law professor (and, as I write, head of the Congressional Oversight Committee) Elizabeth Warren's research from the Consumer Bankruptcy Project shows that the odds of going bankrupt are exponentially greater if you're a single parent, and single parents are much more likely to have lower household incomes. A *Washington Post* story a few years ago dared to blurt out the implications of these findings: that marriage is becoming not only something that the more educated do but something that well-off folks do. After all, college-educated women are half as likely to divorce, possibly because they wait longer to get married and have children (getting married before the age of twenty-five bodes badly for staying married).

Beyond the financial benefits, it seems that the institution of marriage may change your personal behavior for the better—especially men. Men tend to work more after they get married, to help support a spouse and family. There's a lot less reckless behavior (fewer accidents, DUIs, etc.) when men get married. And according to an oft-quoted study by Rand in the 1990s, married men's home life reduces stress, discourages unhealthy behavior, improves nutrition, and includes better care for illnesses. The study also posits that married men in their fifties through seventies lower their mortality rates.

However, married women haven't gained many, if any, of these

64.5 percent of boys
57.6 percent of girls

Number of high school seniors in 2006 who agreed or mostly agreed that "it's usually a good idea to live together before getting married . . . to find out if you really get along."

In 1976, only 44.9 percent of boys and 32.3 percent of girls the same age agreed.

Source: University of Michigan

marriage benefits to health or even wealth. Nearly all of the benefits of marriage are enjoyed by men, turning on its head the old assumption that women marry up or into a better situation. But even though two-thirds of women still make less than their spouse, the trend of women being better educated and earning more or the same as their spouse is growing. More married women now make more or the same as their male spouse than ever. As for women's health, the flip side seems to be the case: Women get fatter when they get married. Personal amens aside, a 2009 obesity study found that married couples are twice as likely to get obese as the nonmarried. But for married men, their risk of obesity tends to go up only in the first few years of marriage, whereas for women, the longer the marriage, the more pounds packed on. But even in the first five years, married women's risk of being overweight is 63 percent higher than unmarried women. When it comes time to shed those dangerous pounds (see "The Real Cost of Bad Habits"), being married comes into play as a motivator. On average, getting fit with a spouse nets you five pounds more lost than going it alone.

But here's the rub: *Positive marriage effects work only if you stay (happily) married.* To gain the benefits of the better health and better wealth of being married, you must be consistently married: not divorced, not cohabiting.

THE REAL COST OF GETTING MARRIED

To many, marriage just seems like a too-pricey proposition. So what if you live longer and eventually have more money if you can't afford the freakin' party in the first place! Researchers at the University of Michigan found that for many cohabiting couples, dread of the cost of getting married (and divorced) gets in the way of a marriage happening in the first place. But, of course, it doesn't have to be that way.

Getting Engaged

Thousands of years ago, the soon-to-be bride was traded for cows or the melding of families and land. Later, we had dowries (in some cultures we still do). As modern as we think we now are, there's still something suspect about the fact that the average cost of an engagement ring continues to be astronomical: In 2009, according to TheKnot.com, the average engagement bauble cost $5,487, falling only 5 percent from the year before. With the average man's income at only a bit above $40,000 a year, this amount is absurd and, we hope, inflated by the top 1 percent of earners who spend into the six figures.

"But I'm worth it!" you say. However, your worth may be better spent on something that actually builds your net worth. I know there's no talking us into not getting a ring (even I'm not immune), but it doesn't have to cost so much. The recommendation of spending

---

two months' salary on an engagement ring is, as the Brits say, bollocks. This amount came from the diamond industry, and surely they didn't have your personal finances in mind when they came to this figure.

- **Save for it and have a budget.** If you buy a $5,000 ring on credit and take four years to pay it back with interest, that's around $6,000 that could have gone to buying a home together two years sooner. A ring or a home? Either save up for the ring with automated savings and wait to get engaged, or get engaged without a ring; it may take you eight months to save up for it (or more), but you'll be free of the damage debt will do.
- **Shop smart.** That blue box? It will cost you nearly double than will a comparable ring from somewhere else. That's a pricy box. What matters when it comes to diamonds are the Cs: cut, color, carat, clarity. Once you know what you're looking for in those four Cs, and as long as you get a legitimate appraisal, you don't have to buy your ring at retail. Buy from estate sales or auction houses, be flexible about styles, avoid high-end retailers, know your diamonds so you don't get duped. In the end, it's literally a rock.
- **Be different.** These days, nontraditional rings are a fantastic option. If I didn't get my diamond estate ring, my husband had as a second choice a huge emerald. Why not? It was beautiful and cost much less than a diamond of comparable size. Be flexible, get creative, and most of all, stick to a (small) budget that doesn't start you both off in a financial hole.

There is no better way to start five lengths behind in the race to build security, stability, and maybe one day, wealth than to start your lives together owing someone, big-time, for a party. But I also realize that there is sometimes no steering the engaged toward a less pricey direction.

Weddings are not rational affairs. Accountants are not usually part of the wedding planning process. Wedding ceremonies can be cultural, religious, all about the extended family, or about only the two of you—sometimes a tradition, sometimes a statement, but in every case, how we get married and how much we spend falls in line with what it means to us personally as well as our available resources. Some parents are willing to foot the full bill, though less than a quarter actually do. About one-third of couples pay for the wedding themselves and the rest pull together a hybrid of money from their wallets, parents, other family, and even friends. But do you have to try to get the *Today* show to pay for your wedding by winning their annual competition or agree to product placement to get everything for free (hello, Star Jones)? Not necessarily.

The average cost of a wedding these days is around $27,000 according to wedding pros at TheKnot.com. If you borrowed $27,000 at a fairly cheap 12 percent interest, how long would it take for you to pay that off? Throw about $500 a month at it and it will take you six years and seven months to pay it off as well as over $12,000 in interest (imagine what you could do with twelve Gs!). This is what I mean about starting behind the line. If instead you spent what you already had in the bank or saved up for it, combining it with maybe some additional funds from family members, you could have a $10,000 wedding with $5,000 coming from you and $5,000 from family— nothing going toward interest payments. Now imagine instead you were putting that same $500 a month away into a Roth IRA to save for a home and you're earning a 5 percent average return. After that same period of six years, you'd have over $42,000. Forty-two *thousand* dollars in six years!

So, put your wedding on a credit card or bank loan and find yourself not only out that $27,000 but $12,000 in interest after six years, and you'll have lost over $42,000 in possible savings.

But I get it. You want and need to have a celebration that brings family together. Eloping to city hall is not for everybody (thank goodness!).

The wise choice is to balance the financial cost with the personal cost of doing a wedding your way. If you accept full payment from the parents, you may have to bow to them when it comes to inviting cousins you haven't seen since you were three years old. But you may be able to have the flashy fiesta you've always dreamed of. Or you can accept partial help and make concessions like giving up a few chairs to your parents' coworkers but also find a way to pay out of your pocket without putting yourself too far behind the starting line. Or do as my husband and I did—pay for it all yourselves with saved-up money. Translation: small and casual. We were still out $10,000 for the ceremony and party. Had we eloped, we'd have had more money for other things. But some costs in life are worthwhile.

With so many variants when it comes to marriage and wedding advice, the key to keeping the costs down is to know what you're willing to do without, know (and set) your limits, and fully realize that if you don't put your accounting hat on, the price may be too much in the end.

How far behind the starting line do you want to be once the honeymoon's over?

Real $$$ Cost of Getting Married	Real Personal Cost of Getting Married
Potentially enormous wedding expenses, including ceremony, reception, license (depends on personal choices)	Possible perceived cost of making commitment
Legal change of name (if chosen to do) and change to all government documents such as passports	Possible change of expected roles in relationship
	New family and friends, who may cause stress

Real $$$ Benefits of Getting Married	Real Personal Benefits of Getting Married
Legal rights	Companionship and care for life
Medical rights	Children/nuclear family (if desired)
Estate and tax breaks/rights	Change in societal status
Access to employer benefits	Feelings of security and stability
Insurance discounts	Possible health benefits (such as a longer, healthier life)
Other spending discounts (memberships, etc.)	New family and friends

GETTING UNHITCHED: DIVORCE

I'm not being cynical by putting marriage and divorce together in the same chapter, just practical. After all, you can't get divorced without being married first. And, of course, we would love one (marriage) to happen without the other (divorce). Unfortunately, 40 percent of the time, that's not the case. Get into the nitty-gritty of the costs of both, as well as getting engaged, and it's surprising how many of the costs—and benefits—depend on how we choose to do what we do. There are few lifetime changes that are so much in our control in terms of cost, both financial and personal. But whether you marry at city hall or get a cheap, friendly online divorce, the simple act of blending and/or breaking households has costs and benefits of its own.

The financial cost of divorce can serve as its own deterrent. In some states, everything you earn and own is split between spouses. In other states, it's only what you've earned or owned during the marriage that counts, and if you have a cutthroat lawyer in a state with wobbly divorce laws, you can walk away with everything, except those pricey legal fees, of course. But divorce is not as easy as separating mine and yours, and it can take years for the process to be finalized.

I can attest personally, however, to the well-documented emotional, psychological, and physical costs of divorce. According to the *Journal of Health and Social Behavior*, couples who split have 20 percent more chronic health issues (diabetes, heart disease) than couples who stay happily married. During a divorce and soon afterward, rates of depression and anxiety spike. And even after remarriage, those who divorced never fully recover the immune system health they enjoyed before marriage. The same researchers at the University of Chicago found that people in second marriages had 12 percent more chronic health problems than those who stayed continuously married.

The culprit is stress. Divorce can feel like a death, death of a life-changing relationship. It can also feel like an enormous failure. You not only have to divide your family and bear the strain on your children, but divide extended families (in-laws) and friends and neighbors. There is a list of life stressors that's often used in psychology to rate your level of stress exposure in the past twelve months—it is the Holmes and Rahe Stress Scale developed to predict susceptibility to stress-related illnesses. To give you an idea at just how serious those in the mental health business feel this life event is, at the top of the list as the most stressful life event is "Death of spouse" followed immediately by "Divorce."

How messy and long and acrimonious your divorce is can weigh into just how stressful physically and psychologically the split will be, but also weighing in are reactions of the children, if there are any, and how good your relationship with them is at the time and afterward. Sometimes the psychology of divorce can be more personal than just your relationship with your soon-to-be ex. It can be about your expectations, your hopes and dreams for a family, your age, and your culture or religion. But if you can maintain a civil relationship with your spouse and, if applicable, help your children through the difficult adjustment period, you'll be in better shape and pay a lower personal cost.

Since personal costs when it comes to divorce depend so much on personal factors, such as presence of children, length of marriage, and quality of relationship, the costs of divorce are just that: personal. We do know that no divorce is fun. Surely my divorce from my starter marriage (we were in divorce proceedings longer than we were married), as devastating as it was, pales in comparison to my parents' divorce after a marriage of almost thirty years and after having six children. Just as with death, we all suffer differently and in our own way with divorce; levels of pain, and even relief, are personal.

The financial costs of divorce can seem to cross just as wide a span as a galaxy: from $50 to $50 million. Though most of us realize that divorce is a pricey thing to do—women see their financial status decrease an average of 30 percent while men suffer 10 percent less—many of us may be surprised as to just how deep and wide these costs run. The average divorce now sits around $20,000, fueling a $28 billion industry. And interestingly enough, the rates of divorce in the United States have been continuously going down and/or holding steady since their peak in the 1980s. Why? Most ascribe it to the same culprit that we see in the cost of getting married. Who's getting married? Older, better-educated, higher-income Americans. And what decreases your odds of divorce? Getting married later in life (especially after the age of twenty-seven), being better educated, and having a higher household income. Whether again this means that like is marrying like or some factors feed others (Do well-off people value commitment more? Or is it a matter of the well-off putting more weight on tradition?), what it translates into are some of the lowest divorce rates in decades.

But there is something else fueling the hold-off on divorce: the economy.

> **What Lessens Your Chance of Getting a Divorce?**
>
> - Make over $50,000 a year.
> - Have a child after you get married (rather than before).
> - Be older than twenty-five.
> - Have parents who never divorced.
>
> Source: State of the Union report, 2009

The divorce rate in 2008 fell to 16.9 per 1,000 married women compared to 17.5 the year before, and the *Wall Street Journal* reported that divorces in New York County fell 14 percent in early 2009 and 9 percent in Los Angeles. A matrimonial law group found that 40 percent of their colleagues in 2009 saw divorce filings fall 40 percent. It's all about the markets, baby. The housing market at the same time in some counties saw devastation at the rate of 65 percent or more loss of equity/home value while the stock market tanked retirement accounts anywhere from 38 percent to 68 percent. The unemployment rate—and remember, 75 percent of those laid off were men—also reached more than 10 percent at that time.

In times like these, it makes sense that divorce rates rise and fall with the economy. (Previously, the biggest jump in divorce rates was due to no-fault divorces becoming the norm across the country.) Surely money stress and downtimes lead to more couples wanting to divorce, but when times are tight or one spouse loses a job, how can you afford the legal fees, not to mention shifting from surviving on two incomes to one? The fall of the housing market may be one of the biggest culprits in raising the cost of divorce—raising the cost so high that nearly a quarter of clients seeking divorce may still be living unhappily under the same roof. (*War of the Roses*, anyone?) For example, in the state of Maryland where my brother lives happily with his wife and family (ahem), you must live apart for twelve months if you want an easy divorce as opposed to the most expensive option, a contested divorce.

Let's say my brother's neighbors want to split up. Both work, and they have a daughter in ninth grade. But they bought their home near the height of the housing market, in 2006. It was worth $280,000 and they took out a $220,000 mortgage on the property. But by the time 2009 rolled along, when they wanted to divorce, the home was only worth $175,000 and they still owed $210,000 on the mortgage. They were underwater, owing more on the mortgage than the home was worth. Think of this as the financial equivalent of being under house arrest. You can't just sell and leave because the bank would have to accept a short sale, which happens less than 20 percent of the time. Or if the mortgage lender (assuming there's only one mortgage; if there are two or more, everyone has to agree) is okay with a short sale, you have to find a buyer in a very depressed market. Not only will this Maryland couple have to wait to sell their home, but to file for a voluntary and less expensive divorce, they'll have to find a way to afford to live apart for at least a year. Where's the money going to come from? Husband and wife bought the home and took on the mortgage based on two incomes, and neither of them can afford to handle the mortgage on his or her own. Trapped by their home and state.

But does every divorce have to financially destroy you? Not at all. Three things greatly impact the financial cost of divorce:

1. How complicated is your financial life?

- Do you own assets (your home, vacation home, cars, etc.) together?
- Did you earn most of your money before or before the marriage?
- Do you have a trust or estate with proceeds that fall under the marriage?
- Do you own a business or other business interests together?

2. What can you agree on?

- Do you agree on how to split your assets?
- Do you agree on who pays what in terms of alimony and/or settlement?
- Have you worked out who is going to pay how much in child support and/or college costs for the kids?
- Do you agree on who will get full or partial custody?

3. What state is your paperwork in?

- Billable hours for lawyers include digging up paperwork for you; just having all your assets, liabilities, and accounts in order can save you thousands in legal fees.

There are several ways to get a divorce that depend especially on how you answer the first two questions just listed.

DIY Divorce

A do-it-yourself (DIY) divorce is when you head online to legal sites that allow you to fill out the paperwork and file for divorce on your own. If you've been married for a short time, have no children, no joint assets or liabilities, and keep all your finances separate, there's little reason not to DIY. It can run anywhere from $50 to $250.

Uncontested Divorce

You both agree on separation of all assets, debts, children's status, and so on, but things are a bit too complicated for an online, inexpensive divorce. Uncontested divorce can be done without attorneys, which keeps the cost down, but what really keeps money in your pocket is that you won't have to go to court. Every day in divorce court is an expensive day. You can divorce this way for as little as $600 to a couple thousand dollars, depending on your state and requirements.

Mediation

With mediation, you're looking at hiring a professional (usually a lawyer who specializes in mediation) who will work as a third-party mediator for the both of you to get you to agree on certain items. Again, this is all about avoiding going to court. If you have slight disagreements regarding assets, debt, or the children but you're for the most part friendly to each other, a mediator will cost much less than each of you hiring lawyers individually. You're heading into the thousands of dollars, but closer to $5,000 than $50,000.

Contested Divorce

If you cannot agree on division of property, debts, or responsibility regarding the children, you've got yourself the priciest divorce option. A contested divorce means two lawyers (or more), two possibly very big bills, not to mention days in court contesting each other. The sky's the limit when it comes to what a contested divorce can cost. It's possible to have a contested divorce drag on for years and rack up hundreds of thousands in billable hours. Lawyers tend to cost $75 to $450 an hour, and many require up-front retainers of anywhere from $500 to thousands of dollars.

THE AFTERMATH

With marriage, you have the initial cost of the proceedings (wedding), then you reap the benefits; with divorce, you also have the cost of the proceedings, but it's followed by a period of even more cost. Depending on what state you got married in, what state you lived in together as a married couple, and what state you get divorced in, there are myriad rules as to how your assets, liabilities, and responsibilities are split. For example, one of the most common questions I get from people undergoing the process is who's responsible for whose credit card debt? It depends on the state. There are still eight states that say that *all* debt, no matter which spouse racked it up, is the responsibility of both spouses—a horrifying proposition in relationships where one spouse has a problem with credit cards. However, there are other states where the debt belongs to the spouse who borrowed it. Either way, it's very important with the costs during and after a divorce to pay close attention to the repercussions of your split—both for your sanity and your wallet.

Keep in mind the following and don't let your lawyer or mediator (if you have one) forget to address each—the sooner the better, and the cheaper.

- **Debts.** Who will be responsible for which debts including student loans incurred before the marriage and within the marriage as well as credit cards? If you have joint credit cards, you will both be responsible for the debt, no matter which state you live in. However, if you have separate cards and accounts, only in some states will you be liable for all debts. If your spouse is an authorized user, you are fully responsible for all charges as the main account holder. If it's a mortgage or second mortgage, the debt will be assumed by whoever gets custody of the home, but if you want to split the equity in the home, you may have to sell to cancel the debt, or buy out your spouse.
- **Health insurance.** Until new healthcare plans kick in requiring us all to have insurance, one of the biggest dangers is to end up going without insurance after a divorce because you can no longer be on your ex's policy. You can, however, ask in the divorce proceedings, especially if you're a spouse who has not worked while taking care of the home, to continue coverage under your ex's plan until you are remarried. And have a plan in place if he

or she loses a job and coverage and/or changes jobs, which may mean that you lose coverage. Do not let this expense creep up on you or go without coverage. The costs can be enormous and even put you into bankruptcy.

- **Estate plans and beneficiaries.** Change your will and trusts to reflect your new family structure. If you no longer want your assets going to your ex when you pass away, the divorce does not change that in your will, only you can. Also, review all insurance policies and change your beneficiaries if you need, or wish, to do so. Again, divorce does not change who gets the proceeds of your estate or insurance when you pass away. The paperwork can run deep, but it's important to be aware and review.

- **Assets.** How can assets cost you? Well, if you get awarded only assets held in IRAs or other retirement accounts, you may have a lot less cash than you thought to live off of. If you solely get assets held in tax shelters, realize that you'll pay penalties and taxes if you withdraw before retirement/you qualify. Have a plan in place to adjust your living arrangements if you're left without a cash flow and know your options (such as a Qualified Domestic Relations Order; see the IRS's website at www.irs.gov).

- **Social Security.** Will you be entitled to your ex's Social Security after the divorce? If so, how much? If you can, find out your ex's Social Security schedule, because waiting just a month or more to file for divorce could mean a difference in thousands of dollars in Social Security payments to you. This can be a substantially important piece of information, especially if you'll be depending on these payments soon.

- **Taxes.** Filing for divorce can affect your taxes substantially. If your taxes have been determined based on filing jointly, what will happen come tax time if your ex files separately but you haven't made withholding adjustments? Talk to an accountant as well as your lawyer on this one or do the research yourself as to how and when you need to make changes to your tax filing status and withholding so you're not surprised by a tax bill you didn't see coming. Also, watch out for taxes when you split assets such as investments that are subject to capital gains tax.

- **Moving and other surprise expenses.** Don't underestimate the cost of physically separating yourselves from each other. Moving doesn't necessarily stop with putting your things under a new roof, security deposits, and so on, but changing titles on cars and homes, placing children in new schools, managing a new commute, and suddenly doing this all on one income or solely on income from the divorce. Did your spouse also take care of repairs at home? Will you have to hire someone to help with certain household duties? And what about helping to pay for the kids' college? Who's going to be responsible? Where will the family pets go and who will pay for vet bills? Take a week to write down every responsibility you each have as well as those you see in the future. The more you get clear now, the less the chance that you'll end up back in court, racking up more costs.

Being vigilant about paperwork is key. And if you think being angry and vengeful feels good now, know that it will cost you the most in terms of legal costs. As I'm familiar with some of the difficulties of separating emotions from money when it comes to divorce, the more you can think about your long-term financial and physical health, rather than enacting cold, financial vengeance now, the better off you (and your kids) will be and the less divorce will cost you in every way.

But sometimes the financial costs are personally well worthwhile. I know that the $1,200 I spent that I didn't have (in the slightest!) to get out of a six-month marriage was worth it a hundred times over. Even if divorce will cost you tremendously, no matter how much you try to be amicable and keep costs low, know that the personal gains in happiness and your emotional health (which affects your physical health) can be worth every penny. That includes a happier home environment (happy parent = happy home) for any children involved. The exorbitant financial costs and emotional distress of divorce can be greatly outweighed by not only your own eventual happiness and fulfillment but that of other friends, family, and your children as well. You can change your life significantly after divorce, including finding another, more suitable partner. There is a light at the end of the cost tunnel of divorce, as long as you keep it in sight.

To Pre-Nup or Not to Pre-Nup?

If you're looking to save money on divorce fees, is a prenuptial agreement before you get married the answer? Pre-nups cost money to put together, and most important, they can be overruled by the courts. Having a pre-nup is not an ironclad guarantee that you won't have to go to court if and when you divorce. So, does it make sense?

Starting a supposedly lifelong commitment to someone by presenting him or her with a document that presumes an end to the marriage may not bode well for the marriage. However, if you come into a marriage with large familial assets that your family wants to protect, a pre-nup may make them feel better. Or if you have come into the marriage with substantial assets that you've earned on your own and you don't want your significant other to be able to take half when he or she decides to run away with a young paramour, it may make sense for you.

The cost of pre-nups may or may not save you on the cost of divorce but if the benefit is more than financial—it's personal—it may be worth the cost, no matter what happens in the courts.

Postnuptial agreements are also around these days—when you build a legal agreement within a marriage to protect your assets. If you're wealthy enough to even consider making these moves and you're okay with the implications to your marriage, at least take the time to meet with an attorney or two to advise you on your best approach.

Real $$$ Cost of Divorce	Real Personal Cost of Divorce
Legal proceedings (ranging from $500 to millions)	Distress over legal proceedings and possibly acrimonious proceedings
Sale and split of assets/property such as home(s), retirement accounts	Distress over loss of property/assets
Loss of full joint income	Distress over possible relocation and/or custody arrangements
Loss of marital benefits (such as insurance)	Potential feelings of failure
Loss of possible tax advantages	Change in marital/society status—stigma
Possible relocation costs	Potential loss of in-law family contact and/or formerly mutual friends

The Real Cost of Living

Real $$$ Benefits of Divorce	Real Personal Benefits of Divorce
Future gains from potential freedom to pursue other professional/career interests	Freedom from a possibly untenable, distressful household situation/relationship
	Freedom from a possibly damaging relationship to/for children involved
	Freedom to seek alternate mate/partner
	Possibly improved stress levels , physical health, and happiness over time

The Real Cost of
Family

*Building and caring for a family has a
high price, but the return is priceless.*

I had just finished paying the monthly bills. Dazed, I walked into the kitchen for some lunch. My husband popped in for the same. Noticing my shell-shocked face he asked, "Oh, honey, what's wrong?" I wrapped my arms around him and broke down in tears. We had $500 left in the bank. And I was five months pregnant.

Let's not pretend that having kids is a rational process. Or that there really is a good time to have kids, or that you'll ever be truly, perfectly financially ready. You can plan as much as you want, have the spouse or partner you want, the job you want, cash in the bank, but then there's Mother Nature. The chances of everything cooperating to culminate in your perfect family as well as perfect career and checkbook are slimmer than we'd like. Sometimes we have to make do with what nature and our hard work gets us even if the timing isn't right. But we can try to plan by weighing the costs and the benefits of where we're at or will be. And in order to plan well, you have to know the costs.

My husband and I had decided to go out on our own as freelancers to pursue both happiness and better, more worthwhile (both financially and personally) careers after being laid off as full-time employees. Meanwhile, our biological clocks were ticking. I was running into high-risk pregnancy land (which is at/over thirty-five years old), and having never been pregnant before, I had no idea how long it would take to get pregnant. The doctors all said, at your ages, figure a year. Well, we'd certainly be beyond our startup business phase in a year and then the baby wouldn't come for almost another year so why not try now? After all, several of our close friends were embroiled in heartbreaking fertility problems—we'd better get started.

Wouldn't ya know? First try. And we were still a startup. Our savings were dwindling in the bank, payments coming in too slow for invoiced projects, but at least we still had health insurance. We thought we were planning right, but Mother Nature had other plans. We were blessed, but that didn't mean we weren't also stressed about the idea of paying our mortgage every month, keeping the business growing, and taking on the costs of a new baby. Of course, those costs and the entire struggle it takes to pay those costs can be more worthwhile than anyone can know.

There is little doubt that our urge to have kids is a biological imperative. Not everyone has it, but most of us do and we should—how else can we prevent ourselves from dying out as a species? It's healthy to want kids, even though they may spell your financial ruin or, at a minimum, cut into your retirement plans. And it's not all about biology. For example, what if you want kids because you don't want to get old alone? Or maybe you just think that it's what you do when you fall in love. It may be part of your religion to not get in the way of nature once you're married. Or maybe you didn't know you wanted kids until you had one. It's about psychology, sociology, and all the other "-ologies" that encompass our day-to-day lives and contribute to our happiness and fulfillment. Kids fill us up as much as they drag us down. Family is family, sometimes no matter what the cost.

As much as I loathe reporting the sad news that study after study shows that happiness and marital satisfaction plunges after a baby arrives, that's the scoop. I, and many parents, can attest to the stress and strain that a new baby can put on a marriage let alone a career, a household, and your health. But that's not really the point, is it? We absorb all these costs because we must—we need and want to be parents, no matter the cost.

But knowing the costs of having kids can help us at least plan for what's in our control and give us a heads-up to prepare for what's out of our control.

THE REAL COST OF HAVING KIDS

On the personal front, you will lose time. Time to yourself, time to sleep, leisure time, friend time, networking time, and pretty much any other time you can think of. The biggest personal cost—if your child is born healthy—is time. (If your child is not born healthy or if you have health complications from the birth, you'll have much more on your mind than lost time. The cost of time is a privileged cost, no doubt.)

Studies lately have tried to quantify the cost of lost time for parents. The National Poverty Center undertook a grand attempt to try to assess these factors in "Time and the Cost of Children." What the study was looking to do was address the fact that we often talk about the financial costs of children (more to come) as well as the costs on our relationships, but since in work, time is money, what about *that* cost? The study found that mothers saw the biggest loss of personal and leisure time when their kids were newborn to two years old, and the time cost nearly doubled with two children, rather than one; but then time costs went down when there are three or more kids in a household. (My friends with three or more kids say: "One feels like you have three; two feel like five, and three kids feel like one and a half.") Dads too saw a drop in personal time, though it's nearly two-thirds less than for mothers. But another big drop in time cost comes when the child is five to eleven years old. (Something to look forward to for all you parents with little ones.) Moms make up for the cost of lost personal time by devoting more time to the household, while the study found that dads make up for the cost by spending more time at work. And when the children are younger, more of the time-cost burden falls to Mom, but when the kids are older, time costs are more evenly split. When you have two working parents, which is more and more frequent these days, especially due to the Mancession (over 80 percent of all the layoffs in the Great Recession were men; the majority of job growth went to women), the question of who spends more time at work vs. taking care of the household can be fluid over time due to changes in employment or job roles.

> The value of household management has actually been determined by the courts—first in an Iowa case assessing how damages should be determined in the death of a homemaker.

So besides changing diapers, feeding, consoling, entertaining, and teaching our kids during all these lost hours, what else are we doing that's taking up time we used to have before becoming parents? We become *household managers*. We pay more attention and time to meal preparation and planning, bill paying, laundry, shopping, organizing, and so on. A 2009 study in the *Journal of Family Economic Issues* found that we spend an average of just over 1.5 hours a week being household managers. The authors of the study say that this total probably underestimates just how much we're actually doing because we intersperse our household tasks throughout the day (and night).

It is surprising, considering how productive we are as a nation and how many hours both men and women devote to work, that the news from the world of family economics has found that we're also spending more time with our children than we have in decades. Why and how are we spending more time on childcare when our job and career demands have only gone up? According to the National Bureau of Economic Research (NBER), in the 2009 study titled "The Rug Rat Race," we started spending more time with the kids in the mid-1990s. And the biggest increases in childcare were seen in college-educated parents with older children. The effort, according to the NBER, is . . . drum roll, please . . . because they're trying to get their kids into better colleges. Non-college-educated parents are also looking to increase the odds that their kids will get into the best college they can so they can earn more themselves. This cost is all about return—the return our kids will get as working adults. We're investing in the futures of their paychecks.

. . .

71

Funny how raising kids can feel like it has nothing to do with money, even though it really does. Even more interesting is that when you try to have kids around good financial times, but it doesn't work out that way (see us with $500 and a five-month belly), you still find a way to make it work. That month of the depleted savings and distending belly turned out just fine. Checks started coming in, and we lived lean—we had to—even after our daughter's first year. But every stretched penny was worth it, both for our business and for our daughter. If we had waited until we had more money in the bank and the business was up and running, would she be better off? Would we? Would we have been able to have a baby? And *that particular* baby? Probably not. There were other, less quantifiable benefits of her coming along while we were starting up, such as the fact that we were working from home while she was a newborn, and I was able to work full-time around her sleeping/feeding schedule, on my terms.

But babies cost money. Knowing just how much they cost can help us plan for them or plan to wait another year or two. And if we know that the odds are stacked against us for some reason, knowing what those odds are can help light that fire under our butts to be more frugal and plan even more for what we can control, such as spending, insurance, and school. The National Poverty Center calculated that a couple with two children requires an income 2.7 times greater than a couple with no children in order for the adults to have the same quality of life. And you may have heard the calculation that raising a child to the age of eighteen costs over $180,000 (and then college hits). But it's the first year of life that's the biggest financial shocker for most new parents. Hence the baby shower.

Add 'Em Up . . . New-Baby Costs

Biggest. Childcare (this can be your second-largest expense after your housing costs; averages over $10,000 per child per year for full-time care).

Essentials. Food, clothing, diapers, medical costs/medicines, car seat, stroller, sling, crib, other nursery furniture, activity items (bouncer, play mat, etc.), bathing, and other toiletries.

Not essential but we all do it. Photos, toys, nursery decoration, child-proofing, announcements.

Check out the Baby Costs Calculator at www.babycenter.com.

If you're preparing for the first year of your child's life, you may make peace with the fact that your schedule, your time commitments, and many of your relationships will change. When other people are involved, it's harder to have control over outcomes and cost but you can look to your current budget to see where and how you'll fit in the additional costs of your increased head count. The 2.7-times finding is a realistic gauge. Figure you'll need to find another available third of your household budget to fit in the costs of a child. Where's that extra money going to come from? If you're already strapped and just making ends meet, you may have to make drastic changes to your budget, your way of life, and even where you live. Not planning well for the financial responsibilities of our children can cost much too much.

According to the Consumer Bankruptcy Project (run by an idol of mine, consumer advocate and Harvard professor Elizabeth Warren), married couples with kids are two times as likely to file for bankruptcy than any other group. And as the number of single moms continues to grow while the role remains just as difficult as ever, the project found that having a child is now the single best predictor that a woman will end up in financial collapse (see page 47). Another prediction: One-sixth of single moms will go bankrupt. Why is this the case? Why is the cost of having children so much more of an unmanageable burden for single parents? Because there is no safety net. Imagine the hours spent on household management, plus basic childcare, plus working (all those time costs) spread out between two people. Add to that the advantage of sharing that average of $10,000 to $18,000 cost per year of taking care of a child between two people. And what if there's more than one child? This is not to say that the costs of being a single parent are too high, just that they are much higher, all the more reason why single parents need to be twice as vigilant about parsing out their time and their money.

How can you lessen or better manage the financial costs of kids? If you've been living with a little extra money left over in your budget every month, with every check, you'll be a lot better off than if you're living paycheck to paycheck. If you are already living tight, there are several money moves to consider that will make room in your budget for your bundle of joy:

- **Find more money.** This is the option with the lowest personal cost, the least disruptive to your quality of life. It means cutting down on meals out, remembering to shop with coupons, making fewer purchases, and going after your household expenses with a hacksaw. Pull all your bills and receipts together for one month, add up the numbers into groups (food, utilities, and so on) and see where you can cut back. This is a tried-and-true move that can net you an extra $100 to $400 a month, or more, depending on how large you live.

- **Make more money.** This option has more personal cost because it may mean working harder and more hours, which is especially rough for single parents and parents with newborns, but it can be an answer tailored to your needs. Get creative—maybe you can take on extra work off-hours, on the computer, while the little ones are sleeping. Maybe you have a stash of classic comics or collectibles that you can sell online. Weigh the costs and benefits of bringing in more while being home less.

- **Change your biggest expenses: your home and car.** Tackling the fact that you spend too much on your housing bills (mortgage or rent, plus property taxes and insurance) or car (auto loan payments, gas, insurance, etc.) means some big changes. But sometimes moving to a less expensive area or closer to the office and trading down to a good but not great car can be just what your budget needs. You shouldn't be spending more than 35 percent of your monthly income on your housing costs and around 18 percent on your transportation costs. If the rest of your budget won't budge (you've cut everywhere else you can), changing how much you're paying to live under that roof and drive that car can be an answer. This has a big personal price tag as moving is no fun, but it can yield some of the biggest returns—returns that you desperately need to be financially stable, not only now, but in the future.

Control the Costs of Household Management

Making sure that no one has holes in their socks and the utility bill is paid can make many of us mental. Streamline your manager role to help lower the personal and financial costs of running a household with kids:

- **Treat it like a job.** Take some of the emotion out of the role so you can run it more efficiently. Go at your household budget and shopping behavior like a CEO or, at minimum, an accountant.
- **Automate as much as possible.** Automate your bill paying, savings, and contributions to retirement/college.
- **Merge family calendars.** Every family member's work travel, events, school events, holidays, and deadlines should be in one place.
- **Shop online as much as possible.** Marry certain sites that help you manage better, such as coupon sites and comparison shopping sites. Go with sites that let you view what you've bought previously so you can reshop more easily.
- **Communicate!** Find the best way for your comanager (spouse, partner, relative) and you to know what's going on, together. Emails? The family calendar? A first-of-the-month calendar review? Do it and stick to it. We all can't remember everything told to us while driving in traffic.

OPTING IN OR OPTING OUT

If you're a parent, you've surely been privy to the unbelievable amount of sometimes vitriolic chatter (especially online) surrounding the question of whether a mom should stay home when she has kids or go back to work. And if you're not a parent, consider yourself warned. It can get ugly out there.

Let's first acknowledge that even having the ability to choose between those roles is a privilege. Many parents don't have an option; they both must work to make ends meet. So what do you do if and when you have that choice? Is it really about money or can the decision be about more than that?

I had a wonderfully strong-sounding new mother on my show, agonizing over going back to work. We were in the midst of the deepest recession this country has seen in decades, and though her husband was working, she felt financially insecure due to the enormous layoffs going on around the country. She asked me if it was worthwhile for her to go back to work after having her baby, even if it meant that after taxes, she would basically be paying out what she was bringing in to the caretaker she would have to hire. I asked her if she was looking forward to going back to work. She was surprised that I wasn't talking math and answered, "Yes, I'd love to go back to work, but I just don't see how it makes financial sense." Screw the math, I said in a much cleaner way. If it will make you a happier person, you will be a better mother. Working isn't only about money—it's about fulfillment, careers, vocations, and roles. I also explained to her that if she and her husband were really worried about his job, by going back to work now, she can establish herself so that if he were to lose his job, someone would be making some money to support the family until he became employed again.

If that mom had said that she didn't want to go back to work, that she would be miserable, I would have told her she'd be better off getting creative to find other answers to salve her worries about her husband losing his job to the recession. Going back to work just to be miserable probably wouldn't be worth the personal cost to her happiness and lost time with her child. It doesn't necessarily have to be a full opt in or opt out of the workplace choice for parents. These days there are a tremendous number of ways to make a living that don't require leaving the house and your family from 9:00 a.m. to 5:00 p.m. (or more). Happiness may have a financial cost, but that cost can be well worthwhile.

The data here are in no way a judgment on who does what and why. Terms such as *motherhood penalty* exist to convey the concept of wage discrepancies between moms who work and moms who don't in a shorthand way. The term, however, is a misnomer. Does a mother feel penalized because she has a child? Income may go down but a human being is not a penalty nor is being a mother something to be penalized for. But is there a cost to being a mother who misses work to take care of children? Yes. But that may be a cost you're happily willing to swallow in honor of your choice to stay home with your children.

After all, at a time when women make up the majority of college graduates (54 percent), when 81 percent of wives have the same or more education than their husbands, and when 22 percent of women now make more than their spouse, we are in the midst of a familial sea change. Women make up over half of the American workforce, compared to 38 percent in 1970, according to the Pew Research Center, and 66 percent of women who have children younger than the age of seventeen at home work full- or part-time.

So for the many of us who either opt out of the workforce until the kids are grown or who opt out for half a year or more, how big exactly is this motherhood penalty? Twenty years ago, a study in the *Journal of Laboratory Economics* found that lifetime earnings for women were reduced an average of $22,000 for one child, $43,000 for two, and $64,000 for three. A study from 2001 found a wage penalty of 7 percent for every child an American woman had, while a 2006 study found that mothers in the United States make up to 19 percent less during their lives than working women who do not become mothers.

Pay this no mind. We can be thankful that the wage penalty is eroding as we find new, more family-friendly ways to work (from a home office, for example) and as we wait longer to have children (the average age for a first child is now twenty-five and only 20 percent or less of moms have kids before the age of twenty-six). A University of California study in 2010 found that how much your lifetime income suffers after becoming a mom depends more on *when* you become a mom than the fact that you are now a parent. The researchers found that women who delayed having kids until after the age of twenty-six were able to catch up with their non-mother peers in terms of career and wages. (I want to shout that from the mountaintops; it's wonderful news.) In the past, it was always thought that the simple act of having children meant that you would always be behind nonparents in terms of earnings, even if you didn't take much time off. This study of thirty-five years of data on twenty-two hundred women found that the key to not falling behind in your wages or career was the fact that, after your mid-twenties, you're more likely to have finished your education and have already started on a career track. It's a track that you can hop back on when you're ready.

The bottom line is first of all, do you have a choice to stay home for a while? Can your family keep its current quality of life if you choose to not work? Or are you willing to downsize a bit to stay at home? And how happy will you be either opting in or opting out of a job? I grew up with a mother who really would have preferred to work, but she didn't see it as an option. She was frustrated and unfulfilled, and we six kids definitely felt it. I worked from home with my new baby, saddling up to a mini-desk during feedings and naps, and managed to keep her home for five months before enrolling her in daycare. During this time I suffered such penalty; in fact, it was one of the biggest growth periods of my career. (I also found out that I, like my mother, needed to work to be happy—and sane.)

Weighing the costs of staying at home vs. going back to work should be personal. Weigh your sanity and happiness against and alongside the financial repercussions of taking time to stay home. Calculate just what an unpaid twelve-week (federally mandated for most employers) leave will cost your bank accounts, and work to save up your vacation and personal days so it ends up being more like eight weeks unpaid leave. Also, look realistically at your health insurance situation, retirement benefits, your taxes, and any other work expenses such as commuting costs. It may make more sense for the father to opt out for a while instead. And as we advance in the workplace, more and more dads are making that choice.

Should you decide to stay home for longer to care for your family, realize that not all costs and benefits are financial. The time you spend raising children is a fantastic investment in both their future and yours. You may not see a price tag return on this investment now, but there is no doubt that it exists not only within your four walls but in the greater society as well.

Recognize, however, that if you've been out of the workforce for a while, your skills may have depreciated and you may pay some long-term opportunity costs. It is interesting that the solution to lowering the costs in both ways (personally and professionally) lies in quality of childcare, flexible work schedules, and the ability to work part-time for either parent. The more we women are working full-time, the less we see it as ideal. Ten years ago, 31 percent of women with children younger than four years old preferred full-time work according to Pew, while today, only half that number agree. And moms who stay at home are coming close to working moms in agreeing that part-time work is the answer; 41 percent of at-home moms say that the ideal situation for kids is a mom with a part-time job, whereas 52 percent of working moms agree. In fact, nearly all working moms and at-home moms agree that working full-time is not the best arrangement for the kids. Many men agree that some work is better than none for moms and for kids (45 percent of men say that a mother working part-time or full-time is ideal).

In spite of all the ugliness splayed between the two factions of working and non-working moms, the personal costs of working or staying home are nearly the same. The same number of working moms as at-home moms say that they are very happy with their lives (36 percent). Nearly the same number are very satisfied with their family life (78 percent working, 75 percent at-home). But we all also agree on one negative: that it's more difficult to be a mother today than it was twenty or thirty years ago (70 percent of the public shares this sentiment).

Real $$$ Cost of Not Working Full-Time After Birth of Child	Real Personal Cost of Not Working Full-Time After Birth of Child
Lost wages/income	Adjustment to new role/status
Possible loss of some employer benefits	Loss of daily contact with colleagues (possible feelings of isolation/loneliness)
Possible wage penalty (grows in relation to amount of time out of the workforce)	Loss of face time with higher-ups
	Anxiety over lost time at the office
	Possible distress/concern over household finances/loss of income

Real $$$ Benefits of Not Working Full-Time After Birth of Child	Real Personal Benefits of Not Working Full-Time After Birth of Child
Save substantially on childcare costs	Ability to be fully engaged and involved in child rearing and household management
Save on transportation/commuting costs	More control over family plans and child rearing
Possible freedom to explore new, more lucrative career opportunities	Possibly lower stress levels than if juggling work and home
Ability to find alternative income streams via part-time work or working from home	Ability to maintain/grow more personal relationships/friendships

Real $$$ Cost of Working Full-Time After Birth of Child	Real Personal Cost of Working Full-Time After Birth of Child
Childcare costs	Distress over not being at home with child
Possible higher transportation costs for commute	Additional demands on time may mean even less time for sleep and/or personal needs
Purchasing work attire	Time constraints can lead to limited/less time for personal relationships/friends

Real $$$ Benefits of Working Full-Time After Birth of Child	Real Personal Benefits of Working Full-Time After Birth of Child
Additional (or main source of) income for household finances, retirement planning, emergencies, and discretionary income	Personal fulfillment; ability to continue career goals
Lessened to no wage penalty	Maintenance and building of extended network of colleagues
Ability to stay on track to increase pay over time/get promotions/build a business	Lessened anxiety over family finances

Adoption

The average cost of adopting within the United States as of 2009, according to the *Adoption Guide*'s annual survey, was around $27,000; if you add in travel costs, that number is closer to $35,000. An international adoption can be less expensive but once you add on travel costs (for example, to China), the numbers can go as high as $50,000. Adopting a foster child in the United States is several thousand dollars in comparison. Adoption is an emotionally filled process with its own types of stress. But just as with biological children, the result is worth every penny; there really is no price tag on the personal benefits of being a parent. However, if you go into debt to adopt, be especially aware of the additional drag on your finances, and plan accordingly not only for the expenses already paid and owed but for the costs once the child is home.

IT DOESN'T END WITH THE NURSERY

My cabdriver Manny was very happy to have a money expert in his car, as he had a few questions for me, but he was even happier that I shared a heritage with his daughter who was in high school, getting ready to apply to colleges. I was thrilled for him and his daughter and very proud of how hard they worked toward their goals. But he burst my bubble when he told me how he was going to pay for school: He was going to mortgage his house! He was going to take every bit of equity out of the house that he and his wife had been paying a mortgage on for twenty years to pay his daughter's tuition bills. I had to ask him to pull over, meter running. What kind of retirement savings do you and your wife have? I asked. Not much, he answered. I told him, I want you to encourage your daughter to go to school, even help her a little bit with money, but do not mortgage all the equity in your home for her tuition. Does she know that you also expect her to take care of you when you can't work anymore or when you re-

> Economists say that today's generation of young adults is the first *ever* in this country that will be worse off financially than their parents.

tire? Who is going to help you and your wife? Your daughter has many more years to pay off student loans than you and your wife have to pay off that new mortgage.

For many people, it's understandable and normal to throw everything you can at your kids so they can go to college and get that degree. After all, they'll take care of you when you get old, right? And what about after college? Does financing your kids end there? Well, we may all wish that that's the case, but the reality is that with an unemployment level twice as high as the general population (the highest unemployment number—46 percent—of sixteen- to twenty-four-year-olds since the Bureau of Labor Statistics began gathering data in 1948), twenty-somethings are coming back home to their parents in record numbers, and rarely at no cost. Even employed adult children are living with their parents. A Pew Research Center survey in 2009 found that the largest group of grown kids living back at home with their parents (about half of all boomerang kids) actually have full- or part-time work. A quarter of these kids are unemployed, and about 20 percent are full-time students; 2009 was a rough year for both parents and grown children. The study also found that 13 percent of parents said that one of their adult sons or daughters moved back home that year. I heard from many of those parents. Some were having trouble dealing with one kid coming back, but many others were absorbing whole families: their grown child along with a spouse/partner and their child or children, usually due to layoffs.

This is one slice of bread for those who are in the sandwich years: parents sandwiched between their own needs to save for retirement and pay off their own debts, while supporting their kids after college, or aging parents, or both. Yes, there are costs involved in continuing to support your kids when they're adults, and even if we accept these costs because we want to support them, you need to make sure that you don't pay too high a price. The better off you are financially, the more likely you are to give money to your kids or provide them with a home and other benefits into adulthood. But there are many parents, and I heard from hundreds of them, who are under financial stress themselves but just can't say no to their kids. Why should they or why should you? And when?

Anywhere from 25 percent to 40 percent of American parents have given a loan, gift, or other financial assistance to an adult child. (Economists and researchers call this a "financial transfer of wealth.") At what cost? Let's take Manny. If he would have taken out a thirty-year $80,000 mortgage on his home at 5.5 percent (leaving $40,000 of the original mortgage scheduled to be paid off in ten years), he and his wife would have $454 a month now going toward debt instead of saving for their retirement. They would have turned an asset into a liability that costs a lot more than what they're currently paying in interest. They could have been mortgage-free in ten years; now they wouldn't be even halfway done paying off this new mortgage in twenty years. Sure, we can hope that the value of their home will grow and that they could even sell in ten years for a profit, but then what? Would they buy again for a cost or rent? Being without a mortgage or housing payment in retirement is very helpful to your bottom line and ability to maintain your quality of life. And for Manny, with very little in retirement savings, if he still has a mortgage in twenty-five years, he won't be able to stop working, and he'll be seventy-five.

> If helping financially costs too much but your kids are not hearing your no, ask them: **"Do you want me to have to move in with you?"**
>
> That's a definite possibility if mortgaging your present means taking too much from your future.
>
> Most kids won't like that idea . . .

What if, instead, Manny's daughter went to a lower-cost public college for two years, transferred to a higher-cost private school that she prefers, applied for aid and work-study, then took out federal loans totaling $20,000 at a fixed 4 percent? All the while her parents, instead of mortgaging the house, let her live at home for the first two years that she goes to a local public college, then sent her $200 a month for cash expenses or agreed to pay for her books, cafeteria, and cell phone until graduation. Her parents would still be out a couple hundred dollars a month in support, but there would be no interest, the mortgage would be paid off on schedule, and they'd still be able to save for retirement ($200 a month at 7 percent growth for twenty years comes out to over $105,000). She would have a loan to pay off, but one that garnered her better pay because it was attached to a college degree; plus she'd have many, many years to pay it off.

> Make sure your kids have at least **cata-strophic health insurance.** If they cannot get it through an employer, keep them on your plan as long as possible, currently to age twenty-six, then help them shop for afford-able coverage.
>
> The possible costs of not being insured are too high for everyone in the family.

The cost of crippling your retirement plans for your adult children, whether it's over-leveraging yourself to pay for their education or handing over assets to help pay off their debts as adults, can be too high It's too high when the cost of helping jeopardizes your finances and your future. Of course, if a child is sick or there's an emergency, we'd all mortgage ourselves silly to help, but there are other ways to help able-bodied, educated adult children who may just be in a rut, without paying too high a price.

- **Don't enable. Able.** Know when you've got a moocher. If it's a cell phone bill or a student loan payment and you know that your child has a job, goes out with friends frequently, or even travels, say no. "But their credit will be ruined!" you might argue. That's life. Sometimes the best way to learn is through experience. If there are no consequences to not having a budget or spending mindlessly, then nothing will be learned. Paying bills here and there is enabling. If there are grandchildren involved, help in other ways such as baby-sitting, buying them clothes, or paying for their daycare. Sit down with your kids and go over their budgets with them to find money they didn't know they had. It's a lesson that can pay off the rest of their lives.

- **Set boundaries.** People go through hard times and it's understandable that sometimes they really need your help. If you're financially secure and your kid is having a hard time finding a job or has been laid off, help, but with boundaries and limits. Agree that he can live with you, rent-free, for one year. If he finds a job before that one year, he can contribute to the grocery bill (and, always, to keeping the house in order). If you're paying their student loan bills, give them a time limit as to how long you'll do so. Sometimes nothing lights a fire under someone's ass harder than saying, "No, you can't come back home." Of course, you're not going to let them be homeless but you'd be surprised how much harder she'd work if she knew there was no coming back. Or if she's allowed to come back, that she's only got six months to get back on her feet. Boundaries limit the costs to you not only financially but personally.

> The **gratitude dividend:** Adult kids feel more affection for a parent who gives them money.
>
> Source: Longitudinal Study of Generations, University of Southern California

- **Formal agreements for big loans.** Some kids need help with a down payment on a home; actually more and more kids do since more people are entering adulthood with debt. But few of us can part with a five-figure sum as a gift. Set a time frame and a payment schedule as well as a generous interest rate (up to you if you want to make it low and friendly, like 2 percent or a market rate like 6 percent or more). You may be lower on their totem pole of debt as other debts will surely have higher rates, but getting them on a schedule means fewer arguments, a return of your loan, and a limit on the difference between the interest they're paying you subtracted from what you'd be making on that money elsewhere.

The wrong kind of borrowing or gifting of money from you to an adult child also results in a personal cost to them, *dependency*, and a cost to you, *resentment*. The Longitudinal Study of Generations, a full-fledged study that's been going on since 1971 at the University of Southern California, has found that money is a top issue of conflict between parents and adult children. It is interesting that the study found the stronger the bad feelings and conflict, the more likely the parents have been giving money and support. To lessen not only the financial but personal costs of this contentious exchange of dollars, as a parent you must ask yourself, why am I doing this? Is it only about helping or is it about being in control or keeping your power as a parent, your hold? Or is it because you now have an empty nest and you want them to fill it? It can be very difficult to let go of a grown child, and sometimes keeping the money ties is how you keep the tie, period. Unfortunately, this urge can disguise itself as guilt, which can be a selfish motivator. What price are your children paying for your need to keep them dependent? You could be enabling financial cripples, sometimes for life.

Or maybe you resent having to swoop in to help or your other kids are resentful of you for helping out the messed-up one and not helping them. Whenever the drama is caused by something you're in control of—giving financial support—ask yourself if the personal and financial cost to your child, your family, and your future is worthwhile. If the only benefit your child is getting is good credit or the ability to keep up a pricey lifestyle, that may not be reason enough.

OUR PARENTS

The older you get, the more likely you're going to end up taking care of one of your parents. Forty-four percent of Americans between the age of forty-five and fifty-five have both an elderly parent and a child under twenty-one years old living at home with them. My brother and his wife are part of this very big statistic. Alex's mother-in-law has lived with his family for nearly twelve years. She has been a tremendous asset to the family, acting as full-time caretaker for their first child, then for their twins, until they all went to school. But she's aged quickly in those twelve years, and now Alex and his wife are looking at some large healthcare and long-term care costs down the road. We are thankful that, as of now, he and his wife are doing well financially, but he and anyone else who cares for aging parents is scared, and should be. The cost of caring for aging parents is much higher than the costs of taking care of (healthy) children. The average nursing home costs over $70,000 a year, nearly $80,000 annually if you want a private room. Assisted living is about half that, and home health aides run an average of $21 an hour. The National Alliance for Caregiving found that the average monthly spending for a parent in need was $200. And what if, unlike my brother, your parent doesn't live with you or even close by? That average goes up to over $320 a month. In total, according to AARP, caregivers provide $350 billion in care a year.

For many of us there is no decision to make about whether to help an aging parent—we just do it. It is a reality that will only grow as baby boomers age and we all live longer. It helps to know what the possible costs can be, and even better, it helps to know what costs to plan for and how.

The personal costs can be similar to taking care of children, in terms of lost time spent caring for and managing the care of an aging parent, but they can also be very different: What you feel when handling the demands of a baby can deviate far from what you feel when caring for a parent you have a lot of baggage with. It's more likely that you'll feel negative stress and anxiety caring for a parent. This in turn can bleed into the other areas of your life, such as your work and your relationships at home.

When my mother was fading after a two-year battle with cancer, I was concerned about missing work yet again to drive the four hours to see her. I knew I had to do it and was going to do it, but I was also very stressed about how all this time devoted to visiting her and talking to her doctor would reflect on me at the office. Thankfully my immediate boss at the time was also my mentor and dear friend and she said to me: "Carmen, just go. Regret for not being there is worse than what can happen here." She was absolutely right.

Sixty percent of working adults taking care of aging parents ask for flex-time or time off from work. In a perfect world this would not have career repercussions, and there are things you can do to try to lessen the cost of losing work, but if you are an employee, look into the Family and Medical Leave Act through your human resources department to see if you qualify for up to twelve weeks a year in unpaid leave. Many of us hope not to be in this position, but when push comes to shove, most of us choose family. There are ways to lessen the personal costs:

- **Ask for and find help.** Whether it's as simple as asking a neighbor to walk the dog while you're away or your dear friend to watch your son while you deliver some groceries, look to the people around you to help you juggle all the demands. Your community may also have low-cost plans that can help with smaller tasks like those groceries or pickups and drop-offs to doctor appointments. (More on paid-aid services to follow.)
- **Keep communicating.** As with household management and children, keep everyone in the loop as to what you're up to, what you need, where you'll be, and when and how they can help. If you are one of multiple grown kids helping out a parent, see if divvying up various tasks makes more sense than burdening one kid just because he happens to live closer.
- **Don't forget yourself.** It's easy to get overwhelmed when all your time is spent taking care of other people. Put your mask on first. It's no help to your mother or your father if you're overtired, overworked, and overstressed. Figure out what you need to do to lessen the strain to a manageable level and carve out the time to do it.

Talking about money with parents falls right under getting your teeth drilled on the list of difficult experiences. Many aging parents feel as if you were talking about death and that the conversation will somehow make it come more quickly. Yes, talking about their estate or, in more common terms, their money has something to do with when they leave, but it has just as much to do with caring for them when they're alive (but possibly disabled), and it can have a lot to do with you and your money as well. And don't forget the **funeral**. The average funeral and burial costs are now around $8,500, though more and more Americans are leaning toward cremation (around one-third in 2006, projected to be more than 40 percent in 2010), which costs closer to $3,000 to $5,000.

My brother had the unfortunate job of being the executor of our mother's will and all her finances. We knew she wasn't in the best financial shape, but we had no idea just how bad things were. He found several bank accounts, small bits of money spread far and wide, along with debt . . . a lot of debt. Needless to say, nothing was left after her debts were paid, but none of us were looking for that. We had hoped to help her plan better while she was alive. She must have been under tremendous stress, and we could have helped. But she didn't want to talk about it.

If your mom or dad is reluctant to share details of their finances and debts with you, at least make sure that they have a *will and trusts* so the courts don't decide what goes to whom, and their assets don't get taken by estate taxes. Help them find a good estate attorney if they don't have one and ask about a living will—what will happen if they remain alive but incapacitated? And if your parents don't have many assets, it's even more important for them to let you get involved as the costs of their care can and will fall to you.

There are different kinds of living care for aging parents and each type has its own costs. Here are some costs to keep in mind and try to plan for as much as possible:

- **They live on their own.** Many aging parents want to stay right where they are, at home. Who can blame them? But half of seniors will have some physical disability by age eighty-five so even if your mom or dad is at home and fairly able, he or she may need more help than you can give. Look into neighborhood senior services (Google is a godsend here), neighborhood-based retirement programs, and other local nonprofit programs that can help your parents stay in their home longer. Sometimes as little as $35 a month can pay for rides to and from weekly doctor appointments that would cost you too much time. If Mom or Dad lives in a community that has many seniors, it may be a naturally occurring retirement community (NORC) and thus qualify for local program assistance. Twenty-five states have NORC-supportive nonprofit programs, and they're growing (see www.norcblueprint.org). If you have a bit more money in your pockets, you can hire a geriatric-care manager (GCM); these professionals tend to be social workers or nurses with a geriatric specialty. GCMs are usually not covered by insurance so you're looking at $80 to over $200 an hour, but the cost can be worthwhile if you just don't have the time or ability to move your parent into a new home or to take care of a complicated medication regimen (see www.caremanager.org).

- **They come live with you.** Just because she's now as close as your living room doesn't mean that it'll be easier on you or your wallet to take care of Mom. Keep tabs on what you spend out of pocket, adapt the household budget as much as you can, and watch your parent's money and benefits as well. Mom will get a tax deduction for medical expenses, including supplies and prescriptions, so don't empty your pockets without using up her benefits first. (Talk to your accountant about what you can do deduction-wise if you take a parent on as a dependent.) This is not a cold approach but a financial reality—it'll be better for both your finances to take advantage of programs and discounts that seniors qualify for as well as use her benefits. And keep this in mind: You are now an official caregiver, not just a family member doing what's right, and there are programs around to help you (check out www.eldercare.gov and www.familycaregiving101.org). There's also a growth market in senior-living companies who offer care in your home. There are usually initially large membership fees plus monthly fees.

- **Assisted living.** Assisted living facilities are very expensive—up to $37,500 a year, according to MetLife—and the average length of stay is a little under two years. There are also continuing-care retirement communities (CCRCs), which carry pricey initial fees of high five figures to over a $1 million because they care for a parent until they pass away. CCRCs are regulated by your state insurance regulators, so tread carefully and learn what services the CCRC fees cover.

- **Nursing home.** At the top of the cost list in terms of finances, a nursing home stay now averages almost $76,000 a year for a semiprivate room and $85,000 a year for a private room. This is full-service, twenty-four-hour care, hence the hefty price tag. To compare nursing homes, go to www.medicare.gov/nhcompare.

It's key when managing the personal as well as financial costs of care to be resourceful about getting not only the help you need but the right information. Your parent's finances may be tricky and it can make sense to bring in a fee-based certified financial planner (CFP) to give you a holistic look at his or her finances and what to expect for yours. For example, many CFPs will recommend depleting your parent's assets so he or she can qualify for Medicaid. But Medicaid can limit the services that seniors can qualify for. Consider the general advice but also consider the state your mom or dad is in and what kind of care you're looking at down the road.

There are two places both seniors and their adult kids are looking to in order to handle the costs of eldercare: long-term care insurance and reverse mortgages. Neither is cheap. Let's look at the costs:

- **Long-term care insurance.** As I write, there is talk about creating a national form of long-term care (LTC) insurance that would be much less costly than an average of $3,000 a year in premiums, sometimes for care that never ends up being needed. LTC insurance is a dicey topic because it's too expensive for many of us and too expensive to *not* have for others. Whether it's for you or your parents, can either of you afford to pay $3,000 or $4,000 a year in insurance premiums, think you'll live long enough to see the benefit, and have enough money to continue to pay for the insurance before you need it? (Are you fifty and looking at thirty years of payments? Or are your parents sixty and looking at twenty-five years of payments?) If you can't afford that cost every month, and few of us can or should, Medicare does cover some nursing home costs, but only some. LTC insurance for now is a luxury for many.

- **Reverse mortgages.** These constructs were pushed like candy on babies to many aging parents and their kids looking at huge care costs while simultaneously staring at big equity. But a reverse mortgage, which essentially turns the equity you have in your home into monthly monetary payments to you, is an expensive and sometimes risky move. You can expect a reverse mortgage to cost up to 20 percent of your equity in fees, interest, and sometimes commission. And turning the house you own basically back over to the bank (while they send you a monthly check) can be a big risk if we see another downturn in the housing market or if you outlive your reverse mortgage. Make it a last resort if you or your parents want to stay in the home. A less risky and much less expensive move (though more personally wrenching) would be to sell the home and move in with family or a low-rent senior facility and live off of your full equity profit.

The Real Cost of
College

No one can take your education away from you …
but the cost of education can rob you blind.

Who would have ever thought that we'd be questioning the value of a college education? It became the topic de jour in 2010. After all, a college education has been the ticket to guaranteeing the good life in this country for generations. But no more. The Great Recession brought about record unemployment for college grads, coupled with record student debt. So what's the real cost of getting a college education? And is it worth it?

Jill, a stylish and magnetic thirty-year-old college grad, emailed me a question regarding her student loans. She was loaded with $40,000 of debt, a mix of federal and private loans, and really needed to lower her interest rates. I met Jill while supporting her nonprofit organization, Dress for Success, and was amazed at her verve and no-nonsense take. She was obviously very happy with what she does for a living and was fantastic at it, so after steering her in the right direction I was surprised by her response when I asked her if she thought her college degree, and all the debt that came with it, was worth it. Jill's response was a quick and frank: "Not really."

I couldn't have found a more passionate and genuine voice of this generation. "I believed the hype at eighteen. But there was nothing about my four years at that college that led me to this place. It was my own drive, my own smarts, myself, that led me to where I am. The only thing you need to do within those four years is build yourself up as a person, build character, figure out who you are, what you're passionate about. School is a formality." Obviously, this question of the value of her student loan debt and education had been on Jill's mind for a while.

This generation of college grads is the first generation that will do worse, financially, than their parents' generation. The American Dream, extinguished? College degrees became the be-all and end-all of nabbing a professional job, but the past recession wiped out more of those jobs than any other recession. We are a global economy now, constantly evolving. We're competing against not only American college grads but grads around the world. Corporations do business internationally, not just at home. Our economy requires more specialization from us than ever before to guarantee any sort of stable job—and how many of us at eighteen knew that job growth was going to be in the field of geriatric physical therapy? And how many of us know what will be the hot field when our kids are eighteen?

You need a college degree to even get in the door these days, but what if there are fewer open doors? Why burden yourself or your kids with the sometimes outlandish costs of getting that degree if those doors are closed or if there are many other avenues that don't require that pricey degree?

Juxtapose Jill's take with my story. Immigrant parents, big American Dreams. And the only way out of poverty and to counter bigotry was to get an education—it was doctor, lawyer, or CEO for me. To my mother, who had to end her education at age fifteen when she came to this country from the Dominican Republic (had to work right away to help support the family), the biggest thing America had to offer was an education—it was a way out and beyond. We took out loans and applied for scholarships. I worked every break and holiday waiting tables, doing work-study during the school year, while my mother also waited tables to help pay my tuition. The gaping fissure between that drive to get my degree (from both my mother and myself) because of the value it had to us and the questionable value a degree has today is enormous and generation altering.

So how has the cost of a college education—what I've called an investment in you and your future—turned into such a potential loss? And what does it mean for you and your kids?

COLLEGE COSTS: WHY SO HIGH?

Colleges say they need to raise tuition to compete. Many of us buy into the idea that the more a degree, college, or university costs, the better it must be. But how can that be if everyone brags a hefty price tag? (Think of it as product pricing: People tend to project more value on a $60,000 car than a $30,000 one.) On average, college costs have gone up anywhere from 6 percent to 11 percent and more a year, way outpacing inflation and surely eclipsing our income, which has not budged (inflation adjusted) since the 1970s. And you're probably familiar with the frightening numbers that show that in 2010, *tuition and fees* for one year of private four-year college averaged $26,273; for public four-year out of state, $18,548; and in-state public, $7,020. As a parent, I can tell you that those numbers make me swoon, and my potential college grad is fifteen years away from being a freshman.

Demand for degrees has gone up as well, further fueling both the growth of community and technical colleges as well as the raising of tuition. The Census Bureau found that in 2008, 31 percent of twenty-five- to twenty-nine-year-olds had a college degree—a big jump from 27 percent only a year earlier. According to the National Center of Education Statistics, demand for a college education went up 23 percent between 1995 and 2005. However, according to the Economic Policy Institute, the economy's demand for college grads has gone down considerably: to 1.5 percent from 2000 to 2005. *These days, the demand for college degrees is coming from us, not from the economy.* For decades, especially through the 1990s when the economy had the biggest demand for individuals with college degrees (and when I graduated from college), it was both our drive for degrees plus the economy that fueled the system. This time, the demand seems to be coming only from us, the American consumer, contributing to the cost of college going up, especially relative to economic demand.

Many parents were too hard hit during the past recession to help anymore with college costs. Between record unemployment, big debt loads, and their own aging parents, the sandwich generations of baby boomers and Gen Xers are just too strapped to help the kids out, especially compared to their parents' generation. This, combined with the credit boom, which peaked in 2008, led to monster rates of **private lending** for student loans—a Hydra monster of debt if you've ever seen one. (More on the real cost of private student loans to come.)

But possibly the biggest reason college costs have gone up so much is their *lagging return*. The middling pay and lack of jobs available for college grads creates a disparity between investment and return. If college costs have gone up over 20 percent in the past ten years but pay for college grads has gone down over 10 percent, how low can the return go? The benchmark for when college stopped garnering us guaranteed returns seems to be 2001. According to the Census Bureau, the salary of a college-degreed employee is 1.7 percent below the average for 2001 (adjusted for inflation). And today's college students are fully aware that they're taking a big risk by going for a degree. A recent study by the University of California of incoming freshmen found that two-thirds said they had concerns about the ability to pay for their education. They also said that big factors in which school they chose were how much financial aid they got, the cost of the school, and if grads got good jobs. These students also reported the largest parental unemployment numbers in thirty years. Mom and Dad can't help; you're on your own, kids.

> Stanford economist Caroline Hoxby found that:
>
> The return on investment in education at a selective school is similar to the long-term return on stocks . . . However, the effect may be from the students themselves—they are more motivated and talented—which means they may succeed even if they went to a less selective school.
> It's not the degree, but who you are and what you do with it.

Let's be clear, though: **College grads still earn more** than those with just a high school degree or only some college—about $26,000 more a year, on average, over time. But we live at a time when the unemployment levels for college grads are at record highs. The term *boomerang* has become well known; it refers to college grads who choose to go back home to live with their parents because they can't find jobs. Then, when they do find work, they don't make enough to pay back student loans and other debt as well as take care of their living expenses. And according to the College Board, between the four or more lost years of work (while in school) combined with student loan debt, it can take fourteen years for a college graduate to surpass a high school grad in cumulative earnings. But in my book, you don't get a college degree to work only fourteen years; you get a degree to take you through your full career of thirty years or more, until retirement. Still, a sobering stat.

> **College Grads**
>
> The federal government earns more in work-life income tax revenue from grads:
>
> $132,762 more from each person with a bachelor's degree.
>
> $152,942 more from each person with a professional degree.
>
> $301,312 more from each person with a doctoral degree.

Another factor in the climbing cost of college is the fact that *40 percent of college students don't finish their four-year degree within four years*; they take six years or more. And 20 percent of college students who borrow money for their college degree end up dropping out without obtaining that degree—ever. That means that less than half of four-year college students actually graduate in four years. To increase your chances of lower college costs, you have to commit to first getting that degree, then graduating within those four years, or sooner if possible.

It's About More Than Earnings

When I decided to leave school with my master's degree in psychology and head back to publishing, rather than finish a doctorate, a fellow student, referring to my master's, proclaimed, "Well, *that* was a big waste of money!" Not at all, amigo, not at all . . .

It was tremendously worthwhile, not only professionally in terms of being taken more seriously and as more accomplished but also personally. When I was a kid, we lived down the street from a university. My grandmother would say, "If you work hard, you can go there, too!" I had wanted to go to that university as far back as I can remember. It *was* accomplishment; it was my American Dream. The thrill and fulfillment I felt on graduation day eclipsed any notion of cost or employment reality and salaries. To this day, I consider it one of the best things I've ever done, something worth paying nearly $300 a month for what seems like the rest of my life. Irrational? A bit, yes. But does the fact that I put such a high personal value on the degree in comparison to the enormous cost of it lower that perceived cost? Absolutely.

Whether you're considering a degree, or another degree, for yourself or you're peering into what looks like a prohibitively expensive future education for your kids, it's not just personal fulfillment that can reduce the cost of a degree but the fact that that degree offers a return that's not measurable as a salary. According to the Pew Research Center, *college grads are just plain ol' happier!* In their most recent happiness survey, Pew found that 42 percent of college graduates report that they are "very happy" vs. only 30 percent of those with high school degrees. Now, correlation does not equal causation, and obviously there are many other reasons why these results are so. Let's look at the personal return on that degree:

From "How Large Are Returns to Schooling? HINT: Money Isn't Everything" (2009) by the National Bureau of Economic Research:

- Schooling leads to **better decisions** about health, marriage, and parenting.

- Schooling improves **patience** and makes people more **goal oriented** and less likely to engage in risky behavior.
- Schooling improves trust and social interaction and offers substantial **consumption value**.

And these results are pulled separately from what's called the "wealth effect." Meaning the researchers took out the variable of income because there is no doubt that the more money you have, the easier it is to see these benefits. So these results apply to all income levels—low and high.

More than ten years before that study, the Institute for Higher Education Policy (a tad biased, surely) found that college grads enjoy improved quality of life and personal and professional mobility; engage in more hobbies and leisure activities; and are more open minded, rational, and cultured. They also found that college attendance decreases prejudice, enhances social status, and has positive correlations with good health overall and lower mortality rates.

> What we're talking about here is what economists call:
>
> Social capital
> Emotional capital
> Human capital

These benefits can all be qualified as economic commodities you can't see or touch—lifetime well-being and happiness or cultural advances. But what increases the odds that you'll see your education as a cost with a high return and that you'll reap the benefits of that cost? It's all about how you use what you've got, how you plan where you go, and what that degree represents for you.

College costs for you or your children will be higher if you go to school solely because it's what's expected rather than because it's something you want to do for both personal fulfillment and as part of your career strategy. Also, college will cost more if you're not strategic about where to go and how much you really need to spend. Jill admits and accepts that a degree is necessary if only because the job market says so, but she is also convinced that she didn't have to go to a very expensive private school; instead, she should have gone to a local public school, and she'd have $40,000 or more in her pocket, rather than owing that money for years.

Few of us or our kids are willing at seventeen or eighteen to bypass the label of the brand of school and be cool with going to a community or local college. Jill says, "I just wanted to get out [of the house]!" I know I did, too. It's a common feeling. The need to get far away from parents and local friends or culture leads many students into more debt than they'd like, since local public schools are so much less expensive and you can save on room and board by living at home. But if you told that to me at age seventeen, I'd have run screaming for the hills! Jill and I, and surely thousands of others, needed to go away and take on those costs of room and board outside the family home. The value of that initial independence is enormous: It builds self-esteem; autonomy; and myriad other personal, social, and psychological skills that you take with you through your career and that may help you increase your drive or even career direction. And what worked for you and what was important to you when you chose a school may be the same for your kids.

If I had dug deeper with Jill and looked at her time at that expensive school, living on her own, I'd find benefits that mitigate at least some of the cost of not going to a local school and living at home. For me, I lived in a house with six kids. As the oldest of five girls, not only was I expected to be a straight-A student and have a job to pay for

> **College Degrees with the Highest Return/Lowest Long-Term Costs**
>
> Engineering: Has the highest earning power of all degrees, according to the Bureau of Labor Statistics.
>
> Nursing: Has shown a 23 percent job growth, even growing during the Great Recession.
>
> Accounting: Has a starting salary of over $60,000, owing to demands in the finance industry.

clothes, car, and everything else but I was a second mommy, taking care of my little sisters, who then ranged in age from six to eleven. It was a complete shock for me to go to college and live in a dorm on my own. No one to take care of except myself? Let's just say I spent my final three years of school making up for the first year, which I spent partying my ass off. But that too had value. I learned some big lessons, and after that first year, I turned college into a career-making machine. For many kids, there is value in living away from your family while you're in school, even if it costs more, much more. It may be just what you need to become fully an adult.

THE REAL COST OF STUDENT LOANS

Nearly 70 percent of college graduates graduate with debt. Add to this those who go to college and don't finish, but still have debt. The College Board says that the average debt load is about $20,000 and the White House says that there's around $700 billion in student loans outstanding right now. Break down who's got the most debt, and public school graduates ease on by with 38 percent graduating with no debt at all, while only 4 percent of private school grads have no debt and 24 percent owe $40,000 or more.

If you use your degree to its fullest or near fullest and if it carries tremendous personal worth for you and if you have fixed-rate, low-interest loans, then the mound of debt, even in the five or six figures, is worth it. But as much as student loans can be an investment in you and your future, they have a flip side: Student loans can be a prison.

Lowering the Cost

Unless you are a student who is without a doubt able to compete and get slated into a top-tier school with inarguable cache, think realistically about the alternatives to a high-priced, well-known private school. (Many small, lesser-known private schools offer their own form of cache— for example, a Jesuit tradition.) A solid education can come from a local state school, where you can save on room and board as well as enjoy a smaller price tag. Or split your time (and money) between two years at a less expensive school before transferring to a more prestigious school for the last two years. You can also plan on school part-time, rather than full-time or, like my husband did, go to school when good and ready (he got his degree at age thirty, after touring with a rock band for ten years). The more focused and serious you are about your college strategy, whether it's going back to school when you're an adult or planning for the kids, the better off you'll be in terms of saving money on costs as well as getting that return on education sooner. However, if, like me, you or your child feels the need to get out of the house, and get out now, be strategic and realize that living away from home will likely put you or both of you more in debt. But, like me, that additional cost will be well worth the experience.

Free money is also always good and helpful. **Grants** aren't just for top academics. You can get a grant for a particular area of study or for a political affiliation or cultural background. In 2009, about two-thirds of undergraduates received grants averaging over $5,000 each—solid money, especially at a public school. There are dozens of searchable grant databases and resources; consider the work put into researching as getting paid by the hour. If there's proven need, Pell grants (which are purely need based) have gone up in award totals.

Scholarships are another form of free money that all students should love. Employers may have family scholarships, and just as with grants, there are more ways to find scholarships than you can count.

Watch out for fake scholarships and grants, however; they became a top-ten fraud in 2009.

Student loan debt is one of the few debts, like owing the IRS, which cannot be discharged in bankruptcy. Could you imagine the rush to bankruptcy court by all the students starting out with $30,000 salaries who owe $50,000 in school loans? This used to be the case, but bankruptcy law now states that student loans may never be discharged unless the school closes before you get your degree, you've been defrauded by the school, or you've been debilitated by illness or an accident. All the more reason to think ten times over before getting in debt too deep. Some questions to ask: What are the chances that you'll be able to get a job to make your payments? Or if you're a parent of a student, what are their chances of landing a job and being able to afford loan payments? And if he or she can't afford them, are you willing and able to step in and help? What are the realistic odds that the debt will earn itself back

Don't forget to deduct **student loan interest** up to $2,500 if you don't exceed income requirements. For more, see the IRS website (www.irs.gov).

over and over again in increased pay? And it's not just how much money you borrow, but what kind of loans you take out that determines the real cost of borrowing for school.

There are several **types of loans** you can take out to pay for college. I'll discuss them in order from investment deal to deadly.

Federal Loans

Loans made by the federal government either directly or through another lender should *always* be the first place anyone, parents and kids, should look to borrow money for school. These loans offer the best chance of return and low cost because they have the lowest fixed rates (the College Cost Reduction Access Act of 2007 set new rates for Stafford Loans ranging from 3.4 percent to 6.8 percent, depending on when you receive your funds). There's also greater flexibility to repay.

Subsidized federal loans are the cheapest of all because the government pays the interest that builds while you are enrolled, during the grace period after you graduate, and if and when you must take a deferment. With **unsubsidized loans**, federal or not, you've picked a more pricey way to pay. These loans accrue interest while you're in school, during your grace period, and when in deferment.

Flexibility can be worthwhile as far as you can stretch it with federal loans. There are several ways to pay back a loan if and when there's just not enough income to make the minimum payments every month. However, *extending a loan term*, one option, may lower monthly loan payments right now, when it's needed the most, but it can end up costing much, much more over time and should be a last resort. Let's say you have a ten-year loan for $40,000 at 7 percent,

You can sign up for **automated loan payments** from your checking account, and many lenders will agree to discount interest over time, to a max of .25 percent the first year, minus 1 percent over time, a long-term benefit. In the short term, you won't miss a payment, even if you travel. But make sure you always have money in your account so you don't overdraft.

but the monthly payments of $465 are too high, so you look to extend the loan for another ten years. Yes, your monthly payment would be cut to around $310, but you'd end up paying more than twice the interest: $34,463 in interest over twenty years vs. $15,702 in interest over ten years. Steer clear of extended repayment if you can. It's a good example of paying less now only to get reamed later.

There's also *graduated repayment*, which at first has you paying mostly only interest (like an interest-only mortgage), then graduating to higher monthly payments over time. Not as expensive as extended repayment, but if you use this system to drag out your loan another decade or so, the price will add up. Also, once you change the terms of your loan with either graduated or extended repayment, there is no ability to defer the loan or apply for forbearance. That's another price to pay for fiddling with the terms of what's owed.

The College Cost Act also brought about another *income-based repayment plan* for federal loans that can also cost more in the long run, but if you can't make $1,000 a month payments on a $40,000+ loan, then this is the option for you. Income-based repayment caps your monthly loan payments to no more than 10 percent of your discretionary income every month; that means 10 percent of your income after you pay for rent, heat, hot water, transportation, and other essentials. It's a very important option if you've got a low salary but a high debt load. But as FinAid! (www.finaid.org) figured out, income-contingent plans, on average, cost you another 178 percent in interest payments—ouch. However, loans are forgiven in twenty years (in ten years if you are a federal employee). Calculate what your loan would look like under each plan at the FinAid! website.

Loan Deferment and Forgiveness

I had a nurse and her husband as guests on the show who were drowning in student loans and didn't know what to do. The husband was laid off at the beginning of the recession, and they couldn't manage all their expenses plus student loan payments, based solely on the wife's salary. I did a little digging and found that because she had worked in a low-income area and her state had a loan-forgiveness program specifically for nurses in urban hospitals, she was set to apply for forgiveness on $40,000 of her debt, leaving her with only $10,000 remaining. That was a happy day all around—and a very happy couple and host!

> Your lender is not going to tell you about the possibility of loan forgiveness; it's up to you to do the research, so grease those elbows and dig in. It's worth it.

The wife could be grateful she had federal loans. Another cost advantage of federal loans is the possibility of making them go away, even at least for a while. If you find yourself unemployed and unable to make payments at all, you can apply for **economic hardship deferment** or **forbearance**. Both have time limits of three years, and with forbearance, even if your loans are subsidized, interest will build up. (Be aware that loans can grow like weeds while you're away.) **Loan forgiveness** also exists for federal loans, though much is tied to volunteer work and the military, such as AmeriCorps, Peace Corps, or the National Guard. But you don't have to leave home to get loan forgiveness. There are many teaching and nursing programs that allow for loan forgiveness after a certain period of service, especially if you commit to working in low-income communities. These are great programs and well worth considering as you weigh the cost of education. Find more information from the U.S. Department of Education online and keep digging! It could be worth $40,000.

The Most Costly Student Loans of All

Private loans are the bane of the student loan world. They have (much) higher interest rates, variable interest rates, and interest that compounds 24/7, whether you're in school or not or can pay or not. Private loans have no forbearance, no deferment, no forgiveness. If there's a type of student loan that deserves the moniker *financial prison*, this would be it.

Private student loans are a Faustian bargain and one you should try to never sign on to, whether you're a student or parent of a student. Graduate students seem to get into more trouble with private student loans because there's much less financial aid for graduate students, especially for master's degrees, law school, and MBAs. Sallie Mae's going rate on a private loan right now is around 11 percent, practically credit card rates, especially compared to a Stafford Loan's rate of around 6 percent. Imagine you have $20,000 in student loans that you took out your freshman year from a private lender at 11 percent. Let's say your lender is kind enough to give you a reprieve and not demand any payments while you're in school full-time. By the time you graduate, however, four years later, you'll owe around $32,000—*$12,000 more* than you borrowed. Then, if you're lucky enough for the next fifteen years or so to be able to pay at least the minimum every month, you'll tack on another $10,000+ in interest. *So you borrowed $20,000, but it ended up costing you more than twice that, at least $42,000 in total.*

Let's compare that to a federal loan for the same amount but at the subsidized rate of 5.4 percent. Since the balance doesn't compound while you're in school (the government pays the interest), you graduate owing the same amount—the *savings* on a subsidized federal loan over a private loan is $12,000. Then you graduate, and six months later (the grace period when the interest is still paid for) you get your first bill and start paying this sucker off. It will take about nine years and around $5,700 in interest to pay it off if you tackle only the minimum payments. But that would be at a quarter of the cost of a private loan.

What about **consolidation** to lock in a lower rate? Consolidation can be a useful tool when looking to save on costs while also bundling loans into more predictable payments. It does what it sounds like—you apply to have a lender buy all your loans and extend one new loan to you at a lower, fixed rate, but with the characteristics of a private loan: no more deferment, forbearance, or forgiveness. For example, when I graduated from grad school I still had a couple of undergrad loans plus new loans, each at a different interest rate. So I applied to consolidate all my loans into one loan at one rate of 6 percent. Since some of my loans had higher rates (even federal loans used to be closer to 8 percent) and some variable rates, this was a way to ensure both that my rate stayed low and that I had one bill to keep track of, one place to go.

However (and you know that with borrowing there is *always* a "however"), there are *downsides to consolidation* including the fact that even if you had federal loans, you give up the ability to apply for forbearance or deferment or another payment plan. You essentially turn federal loans into private loans with consolidation, but the interest-rate savings can be large, especially if you borrowed a decade or more ago and your interest rate is above 6 percent. Because you give up your ability to pause payments when in financial trouble, only consolidate when you're fairly stable with a source of income. Consolidating a year out of undergrad isn't worth the risk.

How to Lower Your Education Costs

1. Graduate!
2. Graduate in four years.
3. Graduate in less than four years.
4. Get a job ASAP after graduation.*

*The longer you wait (or are unable) to get a full-time, career-minded job after graduation, the farther you fall behind in lifetime earnings, and in recouping the costs.

Hold off for a couple of years, even if it means paying a couple more points in interest. The ability to defer a loan or put it into forbearance is worth the extra cost.

Peer-to-peer (P2P) lending, or social lending, has gained some legs, especially during the recession. Putting your personal information and credit record out there for potential private lenders, such as friends, family, or just strangers interested in helping people out and making a return on an investment, can get interesting. But does it offer any benefits to other forms of lending to pay for school? A P2P loan is still a legal loan, meaning there's no skipping out on it. You'll notice that P2P sites don't advertise and some don't even list student loans; this is because the laws governing repayment of student loans are so much more stringent than any other loan. (Student loans belong in the same category as tax liens, child support, and alimony—heavy stuff.) Because there is a credit check to be done and you need to write up your appeal and plan to pay back the loan, you can't, and shouldn't, hide the fact that you want to borrow for school. You may or may not get fully financed, since the sites ask for a total of how much is owed, and lenders usually commit to giving only a portion of what's needed. A lot of how-much-will-this-cost-me depends on the chances of getting financed, which rest on your appeal, credit history/score, and how much you're asking for. Bad credit means a higher interest rate. So time may pass—too much time—for you to get the funds you need. P2P is a creative way to borrow money, but without time constraints to help with things like getting tuition paid on time, that time gap may cost you too much to pay for school.

Real $$$ Cost of Getting a Four-Year College Degree	Real Personal Cost of Getting a Four-Year College Degree
Tuition (from a few thousand to half a million dollars)	Adjustment to new, more demanding role
Room and board	Academic pressure
Lost earning years	Anxiety over completing degree at desired level and in desired time frame
Possibly large interest payments on student loans	Possible relocation and loss of closeness to friends/family

Real $$$ Benefits of Getting a Four-Year College Degree	Real Personal Benefits of Getting a Four-Year College Degree
Increased earnings over lifetime, possibly substantially increased	Sense of accomplishment/dream fulfillment
	Personal growth/maturity
	Less likely to engage in risky behaviors
	Improved social interaction
	Larger network of friends/acquaintances
	Perceived social status
	Possibly higher quality of life, longer length of life, improved health

THE POTENTIAL GRAD SCHOOL GOUGE

Sue was a parent to a young man who lost his job in the recession and wanted to go to graduate school for his MBA "because there are no jobs out there and there's nothing else to do." Sue called into the show because where was he looking to get the money and support for his MBA? You guessed it. Mom needed someone to back up her "No way!" Well, I certainly did. Going for a graduate degree is a serious and expensive proposition for us normal folks without millions. If it's not well thought out, needed, and desired above all things, you can easily drown in the cost of graduate school. And grad school is becoming a more popular choice for many out-of-work college grads or even thirty-somethings and older looking to get onto another career track or gain an edge in the job market. But it's a pricey way to go.

A quarter of master's degree students borrow more than $40,000; doctoral students, more than $70,000. In addition, a quarter of all professional degree students (doctors, lawyers) leave school with more than $118,000 in debt. That's a lotta clams.

Whether the cost of graduate school is worthwhile has to do with several things:

- Are you going with a stringent purpose? Getting your degree to land a particular job with a high salary, for example, or a passionate devotion to a line of work?
- What is the record of the school in terms of job placement after graduation, and what are the starting salaries?
- Does personal fulfillment outweigh the potentially low salaries available in your line of work?

- What kind of loans are you taking out? Private or federal? Variable or fixed rate?

It's difficult to definitely determine whether the costs of graduate school are worthwhile because there is such a range of employment fields (from lawyers starting at $90,000 salaries to psychology PhDs making $37,000), personal levels of fulfillment, and personalities behind those degrees (from super-go-getters who will do what it takes to earn a six-figure salary to those who are more interested in doing what they love than earning millions).

A fun 2009 paper by Herwig Schlunk, titled "Mamas Don't Let Your Babies Grow Up to Be . . . Lawyers," comes to the same conclusion. You can try all you want to boil down a stock/bond investment analysis on the ROI (return on investment) of law school, for example, but it depends too much on which school, which pay level, and which person.

Just like starting salaries for those with a bachelor's degree, the range of salaries for master's degree recipients is broad. According to PayScale, a senior software engineer with a master's degree can look at a cool $95,000 salary, on average, whereas an elementary school teacher is looking at around $42,000 (though there's that loan forgiveness for teaching at public schools).

But let's be clear: We know that associate degrees pay off (and they cost little as well) and bachelor degrees definitely increase your salary over time, but graduate degrees differ. Getting your master's degree in a field that has absolutely no requirement for one will cost more than in a career for which a master's degree is required to move ahead (think MBA, law school, and so on). But just like your bachelor's degree, focused, strategic attendance and borrowing result in much lower costs for graduate school.

Sue, don't let your son go to grad school . . . without a plan!

The Real Cost of
Bad Habits

*My problem lies in reconciling my
gross habits with my net income.*

—Errol Flynn

I hate to floss my teeth. I cannot stand it.

Despite brushing my teeth three or more times a day, I won't floss but once a month, when I can muster the motivation. All this despite medical evidence that teeth and gums are the source of everything from fatal infections to heart disease to heart attacks. Brushing alone just won't cut it. I realize cognitively that it's important to floss my teeth. I've heard it from every dentist and dental hygienist I've ever had, while the evidence continues to mount that healthy gums and teeth translate into lower overall inflammation of not only gums but also coronary arteries. Floss and live.

The simple act of not having a good health habit may cost me thousands of dollars in treatments and medical and dental care later in life, not to mention the stress and anxiety of potential illness. As I write this, I'm seriously reconsidering my inability to get my floss on.

What deters me is how uncomfortable it is; what does not deter me (yet) is the health data (after all, I brush a lot and get cleanings every four months), but what may get me started are the costs that face me down the road.

The cost of some habits is too high to stomach.

BEING OVERWEIGHT

Obesity is becoming the norm in this country—a very dangerous and expensive norm. It's partially the result of bad eating habits aided and abetted by our corn-syrup-addicted fast-food supersizes and the cheapness of the least healthy grocery choices. *Obesity* is defined by the Centers for Disease Control and Prevention (CDC) as having a body mass index (BMI) of 30 or higher, and being overweight is defined as having a BMI of 25 or higher. We're being supersized at such a rate that experts say that in twenty years, more than half of American adults and the majority of children will be overweight. The costs of carrying too many pounds on your frame have little to do with the cost of the groceries, which are feeding said frame. Yes, cutting down on groceries does save you money (as I'll discuss in a later chapter), but that is merely pocket change compared to the repercussion costs.

> American society has become *obesogenic*, characterized by environments that promote increased food intake, nonhealthful foods, and physical inactivity.
>
> Source: Centers for Disease Control and Prevention, 2010

The first and possibly most expensive costs of obesity have to do with direct and indirect healthcare costs and complications. Being overweight can contribute to many diseases and chronic conditions, including some cancers (breast and colon), diabetes, hypertension, heart disease, high cholesterol, and stroke, and this list contains four of the top six causes of death in the United States. Diabetes itself has dreadful side effects that severely hinder quality of life, such as loss of limbs and blindness not to mention an average cost of $13,000 a year.

And note that more than half of diabetes cases are type 2 diabetes (also called adult onset), which is very preventable through diet and exercise.

> One of every three American children born in 2000 will develop diabetes in his or her lifetime.
>
> Source: *Journal of the American Medical Association*, 2003

So how high can these costs get? As of 2008, the CDC found that healthcare costs in this country were around $147 billion to cover health complications from obesity—over 9 percent of the nation's annual healthcare budget. Some estimate that by 2018, that number will go up to $344 billion for medical expenses for obesity, closer to 21 percent of all healthcare spending. If you break down that price tag, obese Americans pay $1,429 a year more in medical costs than someone who has a BMI below 25; that's 42 percent higher healthcare costs for an individual. If you're overweight or obese, you're also much more likely to take more medication than someone of lower BMI. According to the American Heart Association, obese men spent almost four times more on prescriptions, racking up an extra $700 in drug costs per year. All in all, the medical and healthcare costs of obesity and being overweight are 80 percent of the total amount spent on care for all cancers combined.

How do experts think they can mitigate what seems like an epidemic in healthcare costs (even with reform) and shorter life spans and lower quality of life? The Rand Corporation found that those who are obese or overweight can reduce their healthcare costs by 20 percent to 50 percent by just bringing down their BMI by 10 points. The 2008 CDC study showed a savings of $55 billion if couch potatoes got off the couch. Some experts want to get Americans to make healthier choices, thereby losing weight, by taxing soda—which may come to fruition in New York City as I write. Some New York City restaurants have recently started posting calorie counts, though one study found no positive effects as of yet; in fact, people consumed even more calories (a follow-up study did show the opposite). And, of course, if you're a connoisseur of books such as *The Omnivore's Dilemma* and *Food Rules* by Michael Pollan, you know that one proposed solution is to end our dependence on corn in the form of high-fructose corn syrup, an extremely unhealthy substance that is in everything from fries to ice cream.

> For every $1 spent on employee wellness, company medical costs fall an average of $3.27.
> Source: *Health Affairs*, 2010

The direct costs of carrying too many extra pounds seems stratospheric on their own, but add onto those totals the **indirect costs** of being overweight or obese, and you've got yourself a ripple effect that hits all our wallets.

Your *paycheck* pays the price. Wage discrimination exists as well as hiring discrimination. The majority of respondents in one recent study said that they'd always choose the thinner individual when deciding between two similar job applicants. Employees who are overweight, on average, make $1.25 an hour less than a low-BMI colleague, adding up to a six-figure loss over a career. Women get hit the hardest when it comes to paying a high price at work for being overweight—obese women can make up to 24 percent less than an average-size women while even slightly overweight women make around 6 percent less.

Obesity also costs your company in lost wages due to illness and absenteeism; a 2007 study tallied the total costs to American businesses at $4.3 billion a year. Another study showed nearly $1,000 lost in annual wages due to illness from obesity or being overweight.

Moving extra weight costs more as well. The Engineering Economist says that 272 million gallons more of gas is used every year to fuel the *cars* that carry overweight Americans—that's 39 million more gallons per year for every pound we gain as a country. (Another study says that the total is closer to an extra 9 gallons of fuel and $36 more dollars for gas per year per person annually.) *Airlines*, which continue to have a problem with managing growing American waistlines, say that the obese pay an average of $828 for extra seats over their traveling lifetimes and $275 million more a year on jet fuel.

Clothes cost more (around $500 a year more), and *getting around* costs more—anyone see *Wall*E*? Are we doomed to end up floating around in mini-hovercraft because we're too big to get around? Or are the costs of being unhealthy enough to turn if not individuals' then a nation's food system around? Many experts hope that we're heading toward a major reality check when it comes to obesity. When nearly every child develops diabetes and generations of families experience this chronic disease as a norm, something's gotta give.

So what's the hypothetical price tag of being overweight? Add together the higher annual costs of healthcare and medication ($1,429), wage discrimination ($2,500), travel costs (a conservative $25), and other lifestyle costs such as mobility and clothing ($2,500), and the cost of being overweight is around *$6,454 a year*, or that's $538 a month. Over a lifetime (forty adult years), that's more than $258,000. And had you instead put that $538 a month in your retirement account, earning a moderate average of 6 percent interest, you'd have

$1,082,675. But that's without diabetes or complications. Consider those pricey add-ons, and you're looking at $19,454 a year in total costs—that's $778,160 over a lifetime and over $3 million if that money had been invested.

These dollar amounts don't even come close to the personal price you could pay. You may not be able to run and play with the kids. Diabetes may cost you your sight. (How much would you pay to be able to see again?) Surgeons may have to crack your chest open a couple of times, resulting in months of rehabilitation, disability, and pain. You could have a heart attack before your first child ever graduates from high school. There are so many what-ifs when it comes to being overweight because the health repercussions vary greatly. Some people can live without much medical drama into their eighties, whereas others have a first heart attack at age forty-five. When you gamble with your body and your genetics, you also gamble on the price you pay.

Is the Gym Membership Worth It?

Only if you actually go.

Forty-five million of us spend $19 billion a year on gym memberships. But how many of us actually use that membership (and its fee) to its full effect? Let's say you pay $60 a month, plus a sign-up fee. Is that money well spent?

If you go to the gym only once a week, that $60 per month may not be worth it. You'd be better off showing up to work out on the spot and paying $10 a visit. And you're not working out enough to get the positive physical effects of exercise (yes, something's better than nothing, but once a week is only one rung up from nothing).

But you can get mega-bang for your buck both financially and personally if you go three or more times a week, in effect holding off some very expensive, chronic problems that come with being inactive and aging, including damage to your mental health.

If you're finding it difficult to motivate yourself to go, you may have to spend more to encourage yourself. A new pair of sneakers may get you going for a couple of months, or you can do as I do and download movies and TV shows on your personal media player to watch on the treadmill. Additional cost: $24 a month. Benefit: priceless.

To make this cost worthwhile, know what makes your butt move . . . within reason.

SMOKING

A wonderful guy who works in our apartment building stopped me one day to say, "Carmen, you'd be proud of me. I'm trying to get my money together, but you know what's really been killing me? Cigarettes!" (They're killing him in more ways than he knows.) Ralph was spending almost $200 a month on his cigarette habit—nearly as much as he was spending on food and transportation. I told him if it was going to take him some math and lost dollars to realize that his smoking habit was costing him too much not only health-wise, but hurting his family financially, so be it.

Smokers pay the highest cost of all bad health habits; smoking is the number one preventable cause of death in the United States. Some 440,000 people die every year as a result of smoking. It's one of the most addictive habits out there, but it is a *habit* and not a necessary way of life. Smokers start for many reasons: It's cool, one's friends are doing it, it relieves stress, it keeps one thin. But the insidiousness of smoking is that even if you started for one reason and that reason goes away (you're too old to care what looks cool), you're still smoking. The predilection to addiction is high. Why? Nicotine, the chemical that hooks you to cigarettes (along with the eventual physical memory/habit and feedback you get from the ritual), is actually a natural insecticide. But as billions of us have discovered, a small amount of nicotine, such as you get from smoking a cigarette and now from using nicotine patches, acts as a rather pleasant stimulant to our bodies, and then as a relaxant. How pleasant—you get woken up a bit, are no longer hungry, and then feel relaxed. However, not only is the delivery system for nicotine dangerous (tobacco) but the drug itself has the nasty side effect of raising blood pressure, which is specifically dangerous for those prone to heart attack, heart disease, and/or blood clots. This is one bad habit with an incredibly high cost in terms of our bodies.

It's a cost so high that it's hard to know where to start. Recent television ads want to remind us that we might lose a nose, fingers, toes, or our voice or may start speaking mechanically, forever with a hole in our throats. We'll get strokes, aneurysms, have heart attacks and triple bypasses. If we're pregnant we'll harm our developing babies, have more miscarriages and complicated births, and have potentially low-weight newborns. The by-products of smoking are gruesome and priceless in terms of what we would pay to make sure these things didn't happen. But scare tactics only go so far in thwarting nicotine, the most addictive substance around, more addictive than cocaine (according to some researchers). Strangely enough, what seems to work the best to promote the physical costs and dangers of smoking and discourage the habit is the idea of more wrinkles—the physical cost that actually seems to cost the least.

Let's get the priciest cost out of the way: our life span. We know that smoking shortens your life, but by how much? One study says that every cigarette you smoke (listen in, occasional smokers) cuts eleven minutes off your life. But eleven minutes seems like small change, until you add it up. Smoke a pack a day, that's almost four hours of your life lost a day. In a month, you've shortened your life by four and a half days. In one year, you're out fifty-five days of life—over four months.

An early and probably painful death is an incredible cost. Not to mention those wrinkles. But what about the costs that hit your wallet? Almost $97 billion is spent on the healthcare costs of smoking each year, and the CDC says that another $97 billion is lost in worker productivity. We each pay several hundred dollars in taxes every year to cover these costs, smoker or not.

And dare we get into the price of a pack of cigarettes? Few habits are easier to track in terms of *direct impact* to your wallet. Smoking involves one action (at least in this discussion), which is buying and using cigarettes. Maybe you buy them online from Canada or drive over to Mexico to pick up a few lower-priced packs or you live in New York City and buy local where one pack of cigarettes, due to taxes, costs around $10. If you smoke one pack a day, that's $10 out of your pocket every day. If that $10 a day was put into a basic savings account over the next year, you'd have $3,650 by the end of the year. After ten years, you'd have $36,500. And if you had added that $300 a month to your retirement account instead and earned an average of 7 percent over twenty years, you'd have an additional $159,000 to pad your golden nest egg. (Hear me, Ralph?)

But the indirect financial costs of smoking go much higher than the cost of buying cigarettes. Just as with being overweight, being a smoker costs you in the *workplace*. Several big companies such as Union Pacific, Weyco, and Alaska Airlines will not hire smokers at all. Citing the financial impact on the company (higher insurance premiums, more absenteeism, etc.), these companies say no to smokers on the payroll. Half of the United States has antidiscriminatory laws that do not allow employers to punish you or take into consideration what you do during your personal time but many other states are able to say no to hiring smokers. When it comes to the price you pay as an employee, several sources say

> Some radical opponents of smoking say that smokers should get paid less because they take more breaks during the workday, therefore working fewer hours than nonsmoking employees.

that you can expect to make 4 percent to 11 percent less as a smoker because employers see it as an unattractive, unhealthy, and time-consuming habit, not necessarily a habit that helps you climb the ladder.

A poll by the Society for Human Resource Management found that 5 percent of companies trickle down the *cost of higher health benefits* to smoking employees. But for other companies and employees who pay for their own coverage, strangely enough, health insurance premiums aren't remarkably different between smokers and nonsmokers. You may, however, find yourself out much more in out-of-pocket expenses when it comes to more frequent doctor visits than a nonsmoker (which means more co-pays to pay) as well as spending more on medications to treat the chronic side effects of smoking, such as sinus infections, bronchitis, and chronic obstructive pulmonary disease (COPD).

You're also sure to see the *dentist* more often than a nonsmoker. Cigarettes can cause not only that unsightly smokers' yellow on your teeth (and fingers) but gum disease and other serious, very expensive periodontal disorders and diseases. Only about half of Americans have dental coverage and the number is getting smaller every year as employers ask employees to pay more and more for this benefit. So for most of us, even with insurance, going to the dentist, especially to fix something cosmetic, is going to cost, a lot. In-office teeth whitening runs about $500 a visit, and if you continue to smoke, upkeep can cost you $500 three times a year. Treating chronic issues like gum disease, or even mouth cancers, can run you into the thousands of dollars.

Many smokers may squeak by with similar health benefits and coverage for a similar price as nonsmokers, but when it comes to *life insurance* premiums for smokers, they differ greatly. Prepare yourself for a bit of a shock when you try to buy a life insurance policy—a vital move if you have kids or other dependents. On average, you will pay more than double what a nonsmoker pays in annual premiums. If a healthy nonsmoker has a term policy for twenty years (with $500,000 coverage) that costs $1,200 a year, a smoker will look at a bill closer to $2,500 a year—that's over $200 a month. And, of course, the older you get and the more years you've been smoking, the higher your insurance bill.

You also may miss out on Social Security and potential retirement benefits. A 2004 study in the *British Medical Journal* found that half of all regular smokers died from the habit, and one-quarter died before the age of seventy. The study also found that a smoker's chance of living much over seventy years old was as small as 7 percent. For most Americans, full Social Security benefits don't come about until the age of seventy or seventy-one. Smoking greatly reduces the chances that you'll ever see the money that you've been paying into the system for so long, and if you retire at age sixty-five, you could lose out on another fifteen plus years of your personal retirement funds because odds are you won't necessarily live long enough to enjoy them and continue to grow them. Of course, the largest cost here is personal: If you retire at sixty-five and live only to age seventy, you've missed out on your golden years, reaping the rewards of a lifetime of hard work, watching grandkids grow, and enjoying your hobbies.

If home is where the smoke is, the value of your *home* will suffer. My husband and I managed to buy a home from a smoker for about 10 percent less than market value because the home showed so badly—dank, smelly, tar buildup on everything. We knew that it was going to cost us to paint everything (it took three coats of paint to get rid of the smell) and clean every nook and cranny (windows and kitchen appliances had what looked and felt like a layer of dried maple syrup, which was tar!), and we also benefited from the fact that few people bid on the property because few folks want to deal with a smoker's fixer-upper. It took us a good six months of work and a couple of cleaning services to rid ourselves fully of the smoke, and you can be sure that the previous owners would have loved to have those additional thousands of dollars added to the sale price, but their loss was our gain.

If you smoke continuously in your home, you can expect its value to run anywhere from 2 percent to 15 percent less than comparable properties in your area because it's not only inhospitable and unwelcoming (the smell of home-baked cookies, however, seems to move your home off the market more quickly), but it will cost the new owners to have the smell and tar removed. Your homeowner's insurance policy will cost you more as well. Smoking has a tendency to burn houses down. Insurers know that, so they put the extra cost (and extra odds) onto smokers in the form of pricier insurance premiums (about 10 percent more).

Your *car* will suffer the same fate as your home. Actually, any and all property you own will go down in value due to smoke contamination. You can expect the value of your car at resale to be 5 to 10 percent lower because it will cost to have the car "smoked out." You'll also pay more for auto insurance because smokers are on record as being more prone to car accidents.

As for your other possessions, cleaning costs are the immediate indirect costs. Depending on your line of work, you may be spending a hundred dollars more a month on dry cleaning than a nonsmoker, or it may be as small a cost as running your washer and dryer more often. But, as we know, these little costs can add up in a big way.

Just how much will being a regular smoker cost you? Keeping in mind the quality-of-life issues such as lost time with family and friends due to chronic health problems and/or an earlier death, the numbers paint an expensive picture. A pack-a-day smoker who spends $10 a day on cigarettes, another $1,300 a year in life insurance premiums, plus $1,200 annually in lifestyle costs (such as the dentist, smell, depreciation of car and home), will spend *$6,150 a year* on their habit. That's $246,000 over an adult lifetime (of forty years), and if that money were placed in a savings account earning 1.5 percent, that amount would be $337,210; if it were earning an average of 6 percent in an IRA or other investment, that money would be $1,025,742. This is all without health complications, such as treatment for lung, throat, mouth, and oral cancer, which can add much more in lifetime costs; even with a medical spending cap under healthcare reform, there will be hundreds of thousands gone in lost wages due to an inability to work and/or by going on disability.

CAFFEINE

Years ago, I was a caffeine junkie. (As I write this, I'm trying very hard not to relapse.) In college I was a coffee, tea, and diet soda nut. I'd say that I probably consumed fourteen caffeinated beverages a day. It kept me awake, alert, thinner, and able to take a giant course load along with a work-study job. But, boy, did I feel awful, look awful (green is not my color), and the browning teeth were not doing me any good. I even ended up developing health complications that led to my having to quit cold turkey. The searing withdrawal symptoms should have made it clear to me that caffeine is a real drug, and there's a price to pay for going overboard.

Caffeine is widely known to be the number one psychoactive drug taken around the world. And according to the U.S. Food and Drug Administration (FDA), one out of four drinks consumed by every American is a soda, which most likely contains caffeine. And per the Department of Health and Human Services, soda is the single most consumed food in the United States.

Coffee used to be the most consumed caffeinated beverage in America until 1975, when soda plowed ahead. We now drink only 24.2 gallons of coffee per person per year and 51.5 gallons of soda per person per year. But our addiction to coffee is growing in popularity again. Market exposure (those coffee shops at every corner) is up 20 percent in the past decade, and coffeehouses have doubled their sales.

We've all heard of the "latte effect"—how if you just stopped buying those expensive lattes you'd have so much more money in the bank. Well, I've adjusted my tune a bit because I believe that it's the little luxuries in life that keep us going, as did my daily $4 mocha Frappuccinos when I was an impoverished graduate student. One expensive coffee a day does not a caffeine addict make. Drinking one or two coffee or tea beverages a day is a pleasurable thing to do and gives us just the wake-up call we need in the morning. Caffeine in small doses enhances alertness and even improves short-term memory, and it just tastes good. But consuming more than two or three, max, caffeinated beverages a day is known to affect sleep and wakefulness to the point of disruption. And you know if you're spending more than $4 a day on coffee that your latte is going to cut into your bottom line and your health.

The biggest caffeinated health culprit is sugary soda—the majority of soda consumed in this country. Soda with sugar and caffeine contributes to our being overweight and all the health complications mentioned earlier. Too much coffee and soda can also share some direct effects with smoking, such as brown teeth, gum problems, and tooth decay. Too much caffeine also can bring about or exacerbate hypertension, anxiety disorders, and sleeplessness.

And what about that latte effect or, as I'll call it here, the real cost of caffeine? Let's assume your habit is about a third less than what mine was—seven sodas a day (four purchased in bulk or at the supermarket and three purchased at a vendor or retailer) plus one coffee in the morning at home and one bought at the local coffee shop—your monthly tally would be $240 to feed your caffeine habit. That's a cool $2,880 a year or $115,200 over your lifetime, and $480,348 if you invested that money instead to earn an average of 6 percent. Of course, if you add in the costs of potential diabetes from sugary sodas or side effects of caffeine intoxication, you can easily double your price tag.

DISTRACTED, RECKLESS DRIVING

As a national auto critic, my husband drives cars for a living—almost every new car you can think of. I realized when I decided to happily settle down with the man (who has the best job in the world, according to most guys) that his job was kinda, sorta dangerous. Of course, as the argument for guns goes, it's not the cars that kill, but the drivers. And bad driving habits can make for some very pricey bills.

But driving fast (especially in fast cars) and recklessly has appeal. After all, millions have been spent on the *Fast and Furious* franchise and by automakers like Audi to place its (gorgeous) products—driven off roofs and through windows—into every *Transporter* and *Iron Man* movie. Fast, fun, reckless driving sells cars because it's exciting and sexy. Most of us only fantasize about driving like this, but for those who do or attempt to, there's a price to pay. In a cultural shift, it seems that driving badly has vroomed ahead of driving fast as to what causes the most damage. We're multitasking while driving: texting, talking on the phone, eating, looking for something that fell off the seat, checking the GPS. These activities and more interfere with staying on the road and not killing someone.

Distracted driving is the latest threat on the roads. Nationwide, about 80 percent of all vehicle crashes and 65 percent of near crashes in 2009 involved distracted driving, according to the National Highway Traffic and Safety Administration (NHTSA). Blame the cell phone. We've recently experienced a spate of dramatic and horrific deaths on the road from driving while texting or while on the phone. Enough loss of life that as I write, twenty-three states, as well as Washington, DC, and Guam, have banned all texting while driving, whereas others have also banned talking on the phone without a hands-free device. The University of Utah found that cell phone use while driving, even hands free (it's the talking, not the phone, that is the distraction), delays drivers' reaction time at the same level as if you were driving with an alcohol level of .08, the legal limit. Carnegie Mellon University found that cell phone use while driving reduced the brain's attention span by 37 percent. So even though we've seen overall fatalities reach the lowest level since the 1950s, much has to do with the improved safety features of cars (stability control, air bags, and so on), and it seems that we've found another way to make driving distractingly pricey.

Car accidents of all sorts make you pay, from the highest price (your life and the life of loved ones) to the much lower cost of a new fender and higher auto insurance premiums. We all would prefer to be blessed with only busted fenders in our lifetime, but the CDC calculates one death every forty-five minutes in this country due to drunk drivers. The total cost of all *drunk driving–related accidents* is $51 billion a year. Getting a DUI can land you in the slammer and get your name in the newspaper. Again, the highest price you'd pay would be possibly harming someone else or yourself, and the lowest, a fine. But in between those two extremes is the fact that the arrest has repercussions not only to your own stress levels and that of your family but to your image as a coworker, manager, and colleague. You can hope that your image is all that will need repair, but you may also go without pay for a period of time and possibly get fired, finding it very hard to get another job.

In some states, it takes only one DUI conviction to lose your license for a year and get fined $1,000, and should you nab another DUI, you're looking at three years without a license, mandatory jail time, and up to $10,000 in fines. So without being able to drive at all, how would you get to work? To the grocery store? Car dependent as we are, how much would not being able to drive disrupt and cost your life? There are dozens of aftershock costs to a DUI conviction: from your household to your work to confronting your own judgment to losing your license to taking someone's life. Costs that surely outweigh a $30 cab ride home.

Reckless driving is just another way of saying you're speeding (in some states this means you must be twenty or thirty miles an hour over the speed limit) and/or weaving dangerously through traffic. Just as dangerous as driving while impaired or texting on your phone, reckless driving in most states is a class 2 misdemeanor, punishable by probation, jail time, and fines up to $750. But if you're found to be driving recklessly enough to threaten lives, you'll get hit with a felony and possibly over a year of jail time, probation, and fines up to $150,000.

Whether it's a DUI, speeding tickets, or driving while texting, if you get stopped, you'll see a hike in your auto insurance rates. Of course, with DUIs not only are you looking at the loss of your car for a year but also you won't be able to get insurance for at least a year, and when you do get back behind the wheel, your insurance premiums will remain astronomical until you've gone years without another DUI. Texting and talking on the phone while driving in states with laws against distracted driving will also hike your insurance rates. But even just one speeding ticket can almost double your insurance costs. You won't instantly see a jump in your premium, unless your insurance is up for its annual renewal. Insurance companies look at your record once a year during renewal time and, like credit reports, keep items on record for only a set period of time, usually three years. So if and when tickets appear, be prepared for a doubling or even tripling of your insurance rates, as the NHTSA found that drivers who have gotten one ticket are more likely to be involved in an accident than those who have never gotten a ticket. Insurance companies know these odds and pass down the cost to you. And according to Speeding Ticket Central (www.speedingticketcentral .com), having a teenage driver (or any adult under the age of twenty-three) on your insurance may be one of the costliest decisions you make. They say that even one traffic ticket for a stop sign roll issued to your younger driver can cost you another $1,000 a year in insurance premiums for the three years the ticket stays on record. So though you may need your teen to pick up his younger sister from practice or take himself to his job, if he's not a good driver, the convenience may end up costing you.

Real $$$ Cost of a Bad Habit	Real Personal Cost of a Bad Habit
Thousands to millions lost in potential savings/investments	Death
Increased insurance costs (medical, life, auto)	Cause the death or injury of someone else (distracted driving)
High medical/disability costs not covered by insurance	Potentially life-changing injuries (distracted driving, smoking, obesity)
Lower wages (smoking, obesity)	Loss of limbs, ability to speak (smoking)

Real $$$ Cost of a Bad Habit	Real Personal Cost of a Bad Habit
Possible loss of job opportunities leading to lower wages over time (smoking, obesity)	Cancer (smoking, obesity)
Legal costs and potential lawsuits (distracted driving)	Heart disease and other vascular ailments and all their complications (smoking, obesity)
	Anxiety, sleeplessness (smoking, caffeine)
	Cosmetic ill effects (smoking, obesity, caffeine)
	Loss of relationships (smoking, obesity)
	Discrimination (smoking, obesity)
	Potential loss of job opportunities for personal and professional growth (smoking, obesity)

Real $$$ Benefits of a Bad Habit	Real Personal Benefits of a Bad Habit
Possible temporary ability to concentrate or be more alert on the job	Temporary feelings of alertness and/or euphoria (caffeine, smoking, obesity)
	Reduced appetite (smoking, caffeine)
	Pleasure derived from certain foods/beverages (obesity)
	Feeling of accomplishment/socialization (distracted driving, smoking)

The Real Cost of
Being Your Own Boss

*Sanity and happiness are worth
their high price tags.*

F ew things in life are scarier than both you and your spouse getting laid off in the same year. And you just bought your first home together. And a baby's on the way. Welcome to self-employment! Actually, this was my life about five years ago. My husband and I met at the office, got engaged, and then were let go in a massive couple of rounds of layoffs. (Note to all working couples: Diversify where your paychecks come from!) But he and I shared something else: We had both been miserable at our jobs. So, as much as we were devastated by the loss of pay, benefits, stability, and identity, I took it as a call to arms. Let's go out on our own and make it! We became full-time freelancers, and very successful ones, but not without paying a very high price.

We were at the forefront of gouging layoffs across the country, especially in our industry, for the next four years. Millions of Americans continue to be out of work as I write this, and millions more who do end up finding full-time work won't see the full-time benefits we've all been used to. Times have changed, and the workforce and rules of employment have changed. We are becoming a freelance nation: Some of us are going down fighting, while many of us are embracing the challenge as an opportunity to do what we really want to do, beholden to only our clients and our personal needs. No matter why or how you go into it, becoming your own boss is not for the faint of heart. But the payoff may be so very good, the cost is just one more thing to keep in mind.

There are around forty-two million independent workers in this country now, 30 percent of the American workforce. This is a combined number of various nonemployees classified as independent contractors (24 percent), self-employed (14 percent), temporary workers (7 percent), and part-time workers (44 percent). Add onto these folks small business owners, who numbered nearly thirty million as of 2008. Of course, the I'm-my-own-boss life that my husband lives as a freelance journalist/writer is much different from the I'm-the-boss life my brother has as a franchise owner with a dozen employees. This chapter looks at those of us who start small businesses and make a living as full-time freelancers or independent contractors; from hair-stylists to web designers to housing contractors, the numbers are only getting bigger. And as small business is the big boy at the table (employing almost half of all private-sector employees) and as 52 percent of small businesses are home based, freelancers and home-based business owners can unite in assessing the costs of being one's own boss.

First, some clarity in terms of labels. Legally, and for tax reasons, people who are not full-time employees of any company or business but contract to work for a business or project for pay are called independent contractors (ICs). I'll use IC and freelance interchangeably, though there are some circumstances (legally, taxwise, and sometimes personal preference) in which these terms do not mean the same thing. Whatever you call it, it's all about taking the plunge—one hopes because you want to—into being your own boss and increasing the possibility that you'll do it right because you know the potential costs going in.

IT'S PERSONAL

Few things can test a marriage or partnership as much as suddenly working from home, mere feet from each other, while also raising a child in less than a thousand square feet. It's definitely one of those "If we can do this . . . we can do anything!" trials of life. But for me, the personal cost of it all was well eclipsed by the benefits my husband and I got from our new full-time freelance lives. The extent of how much working for yourself will cost, personally, will depend very much on the personal benefits you'll get. They can be immense, maybe not in numbers but in value and quality of life. To get value, however, it helps to hold the following particular perks dear:

- Independence and autonomy (you don't like to answer to bosses; you don't care for bureaucracy).
- A flexible schedule (you get work done when *you* want to get it done—by or before your deadline).

- Have a passion for what you do (you in essence get to create your career and job).
- Opportunity to make your mark (a Pew Research Center survey noted that 75 percent of the self-employed said a big reason they do what they do is to "feel productive" and 55 percent said to "improve society").

Overall *happiness* is another not-so-easily-measured benefit to being self-employed. The Pew Research Center and dozens of other studies found that *the self-employed are significantly more satisfied with their jobs than are other workers.* About 39 percent of the self-employed said that they were "completely satisfied" with their jobs, compared to 28 percent of those employed by others. Also, the self-employed are less likely to work "just for the paycheck" (38 percent compared to 50 percent of employees). Personal satisfaction is a benefit that is so much bigger than the costs involved in being freelance; it has to be, because the once American and now worldwide dream of working for yourself costs quite a bit.

If you work for yourself, especially if you work from home, and someone says, "Well, you must have plenty of time to _____ [fill the blank with have a coffee, go to the movies, hang out, take a vacation, and so on]," it's normal to want to smack them upside the head. Working for yourself means working probably more than you've ever worked in your life. The average self-employed worker averages fifty-two hours a week at work vs. forty hours or less for the average full-time employee. Work can become consuming because, as your own boss and employer, you perform multiple roles (and there is no escape!). My husband and I worked around the clock, securing clients, marketing ourselves, and keeping up contacts while building up more contacts and producing the best product, all while expanding into other areas and juggling our administrative duties. Whew.

There is little, if any, vacation because every day that you don't work, you're not making money at your business or, if you employ others, you're not there to make sure things go right. And with multiple clients, projects, and deadlines, you can find it very easy to go without time off for months, if not years. *No or little time off*, especially in the first year, may be too high a price for some to pay. For example, though I made sure I didn't have any projects due for a month or so, I finished my last assignment the week before I gave birth. Then, since there's no such thing as paid maternity leave when you work for yourself, I pulled that computer right up to my baby-feeding-on-a-Boppy self just days after she was born and went right back to work. But here's where the flexibility benefit comes in. I was able to keep my newborn home longer because I could work around her napping and feeding schedules, and if and when I needed to travel, my husband was also working from home and able to take over. We also pulled in the help of family and friends and, later on, a fabulous daycare with a very accommodating staff.

Having little time off and feeling the pressure to always be on can be detrimental to your relationships and family, if you live with one. If you work and live by yourself, working around the clock will probably not affect others in your life as much. But once you add in a partner or spouse, children, aging parents, and others who live with you and need you, keeping everyone as well as yourself happy and not running on empty requires discipline and boundaries.

Working from home makes it too easy to feel the pressure to be at that desk, to answer emails and texts from clients right away. But as anyone with a successful home business will tell you, boundaries are essential. Set up no-BlackBerry times, such as at family dinnertime and morning breakfast. Full focus is essential to do anything to its best and utmost, so put the electronics down from 7:00 to 9:00 every evening. Focus on bath time, mealtimes, bedtime, and go back to work when everyone's asleep if you have to, but put well-defined boundaries in place to keep the costs of running your business balanced with the demands of family and home. It isn't worth the financial price of earned business if your child resents you.

You may work more hours, but you also won't have a commute or, if you rent or buy an office space, you'll most likely choose a short commute. Saving on travel time not only adds available working hours (the average commute is almost twelve hours a week!), but you'll save on transportation costs as well. One former commuter I know said she saved $500 a month in gas alone (when gas was $4 a gallon), not to mention the two hours each day on the road.

The biggest personal cost for social types is the lack of interaction. Yes, for most of us, leaving a cubicle is paradise. But what about the lack of contact? Seeing only yourself every day, day in and day out (or in my husband's case, me—not always a good thing), can be incredibly taxing and possibly a danger to your business. *Loneliness* must be met head-on. First, acknowledge not only that it's there, but that you have the ability to do something about it. You can email with people all day, talk to them on the phone, or interact on Facebook and Twitter, but that doesn't replace watercooler chatter. Counter the solo blues, especially initially, with *scheduled, regular interaction*. You don't have to find time to see former coworkers all the time (and you may not want to; it can sometimes be more negative than it's worth) but book at least one or two lunches a week, plus dinner or drinks once a week at a minimum. This is essential for not only continuing to build your network and clients but to keep yourself personally in tip-top shape. Walk to your town's coffee shop at 3:00 p.m. every day and chat up the baristas or go for a run with a group or head to the gym. Whatever you lose in revenue in that hour you will make up in energy and renewed focus when you get back to your work space.

Another cost of going it alone is that some of the people who used to be around you did things for you. There may have been someone to help buy office supplies, a tech team to call on when your computer crashed, even someone to answer your phone. Welcome to Do-It-All-Yourself Land! From making sure there's enough coffee to essential tech support, your former *infrastructure of personnel support will be gone*. You may already outsource your legal needs and accounting, but who's going to fix your computer, especially after regular business hours? Part of the reason that you may find yourself working more than ever is that you'll be spending a lot of time doing things that other people did for you or, if not, searching for people to do those things for you. You must have and find local, flexible tech support. Find the best—and least expensive—websites for buying office supplies, printing up your business cards, and building and maintaining your website and mailing lists—all very costly time-wise and an additional personal stress, but all part of being your own boss.

MONEY

None of us knew how our dear friend Michelle did it. She commuted two hours *each way* every weekday to her full-time job with benefits for two years. And it was a job that had little to do with her passions. We all saw the toll it was taking on her not only socially but physically and mentally as well. So when she came to me looking for permission to quit so she could go freelance to finish her novel, she knew that I was going to ask about money. I knew Michelle needed out of that job with its horrendous commute, no matter how much money and security she was getting from it, but I also knew that having money saved up is key to going out on your own successfully. Thankfully, she was a very frugal spender and had saved up months of cash to cover expenses as well as had some freelance gigs already lined up to supplement the lost income. It may be the wisest or most conservative advice to wish that she had even more saved up (a years' worth of expenses), but she didn't have any children or other family to support and she was a renter, so she had no mortgage or other debts hanging over her head. And sometimes there is nothing like feeling financial pressure to get you working like mad, like you need to. I gave her my blessing with the caveat that she be prepared to run out of money if she didn't get the novel done and sold on time. But having been a former freelancer, she knew the drill. And we both also knew that life is short, and she was suffering. It was a financial risk worth taking.

The financial risks of going out on your own are substantial. After all, that is why most people work for someone else: the security of the income and benefits. The same studies that find that the self-employed are happier with what they do also find that the *self-employed are more financially stressed*. We know it's not all about the money, but on the flip side, many entrepreneurs and freelancers go into business for themselves because they know they can make more money on their own—and many do! On average, entrepreneurs make at least 25 percent more than employees. (Keep in mind, since companies don't have to pay out benefits and taxes on independent contractors, they many times will pay a better per-project rate to a freelancer or small business owner than they do for the comparable hours worked by full-time staff.) So there is money to be made, but there is also a lot of financial planning needed to allay the additional costs of going out on your own.

Even before startup costs, you must deal with the reality that you need savings to pay bills while you wait for your business income to start coming in. You may even take the risk of using retirement money (say in a 401(k) or IRA) to cover initial costs, which can be a worthwhile, if risky, expense, or you could plop down the plastic, as more than 70 percent of the self-employed do to cover gaps in pay. Of course, the best way to start a small business is to do it while you still have a job with benefits so you can counter some of the financial costs of a startup. If you're thinking about going freelance and you currently have a job, there is no better time to continue to build your network so you can tap colleagues as potential clients and so they can get to know the quality of work you are able to put out while you save up as much cash as you can.

What contributes wholeheartedly to the stress of being self-employed is the *disappearance of the biweekly paycheck.* Though you'll be able to keep track of your income—who's contracted you to do what, by when, for how much—you'll have less control than you think regarding when you'll get paid. I once did projects for a behemoth of a company from which it was torture to get what was owed. It once took five months to get paid! This may happen to you more than you like or more than you're prepared for. **Ask for contracts that clearly state due dates and acceptance dates for projects as well as pay-by dates.** Submit invoices to receive payment within thirty days of acceptance of the project or from the date the project goes live. Even better, if you can—because it's always better to get cash flowing in as soon as possible—ask for a deposit on the project up front, before your work starts.

Accounting

Sporadic pay means you must live low—below your means—to not rack up debt.

You're going to have good months and bad months. Money from the good months must take care of you during the bad months.

Build up as much in cash savings as you can, more than you had when employed—especially if you have a mortgage. It will come in handy should your business hit hard times.

You will now be your own payroll administrator so put on your hard hat and rally for your pay. Always get deals in writing, contracts as much as possible, and develop a system to track your invoices, setting calendar notices for when you're expecting payment on a project. Find out who the correct contact is in regard to inquiring about payments—it's probably someone other than your project contact. And don't ever feel shy or bad about having to harangue accounts receivable to get your money, especially after sixty days. After all, you worked for it, it's owed to you, and legally it's yours.

Should it be your goal to just replicate the salary you once had? Nope. *Your salary was only two-thirds of your actual pay*—your benefits (medical, dental, vision, disability, life insurance, plus retirement accounts) add up to anywhere from 25 to 33 percent of your full, real pay. Consider that you may need to take your salary and increase it by 25 to 33 percent to live the same quality of life. You'll need to pay for your own health insurance (shop around: Freelancers Union, your state insurers office, and online), life insurance (if you have children and/or other dependents), and retirement benefits. Add on the fact that you'll also become your own human resources administrator, insurance broker, and retirement planner. If you don't take on this role as soon as you're on your own, the cost can be high enough to bankrupt you.

You must take care of **medical coverage** ASAP, and as I write, the national plan to cover the uninsured won't go into full effect until 2013. So whether you pay for subsidized COBRA benefits for a while or join a union for reduced-cost benefits (the best and least costly idea) or go directly to an insurance broker to pay out of pocket, you *must* get coverage for yourself and your family—don't risk your livelihood by being one of the 40 percent of self-employed who don't have coverage.

And if you've never paid for your own medical coverage, until the national options begin in 2013, prepare your budget for a shock. Coverage under COBRA without a subsidy can run to over $1,200 a month for a family of three, over $500 for an individual. Even coverage through a union is costly: around $850 or more for a family of three. The costliest risk, of course, is an accident, injury, or illness taking place while you're without coverage. The danger is too great, Murphy's Law holds too much influence, and shopping around for insurance is worth every pricey minute you're not earning money.

Don't ignore your *retirement benefits* either. Though it may not be at the top of your mind as you start up your business, don't go longer than six months without paying attention. A 2006 survey found that one-third of the self-employed were saving less than $1,000 total for retirement, half less than $10,000, and two-thirds less than $30,000. Unless you're a twenty-something just making ends meet with no family to support, those numbers don't hold. Yes, you need to focus on the present—being able to pay your rent or mortgage—but don't make not planning for the future cost you too much.

When I talk to first-time freelancers, I'm always in awe of the fact that so many don't have *a lawyer and an accountant.* It may be just you in your pajamas proofreading or taping up boxes of yummy handmade skin cream, so you think, well, why do I need them? Plus I can't afford them! You can't *not* afford them. Having both a lawyer and accountant on hand will save you so much money over time, you'll recoup whatever you put out, and then some. Ask around for local references—your community bank can help.

The lawyer will take care of the first step and an initial financial cost that is well worth the price of admission: to figure out what form of business you need to be to maximize the advantages of being your own boss. Whether you're going to be an LLC, an S-Corp, or a sole proprietor, your *legal and tax designation* does three very important things:

Independent contractors (freelancers) and small businesses tend to get audited by the IRS at a higher rate than employees. To lessen your chances of getting audited (which costs way too much time and distress, not to mention possibly money):

- Don't underreport your income.
- Don't overreport home office or entertainment deductions.
- Make sure your tax filings are completed correctly and signed.

- **Protects your personal assets.** Let's say someone gets a horrible rash from your creams, and they sue you for damages and win. An LLC protects you from taking a personal hit for the financial damages—for example, you will not lose your home to pay the settlement because the company is responsible, not you personally.

- **Affects your taxes.** You'll be taxed *differently and advantageously* because you'll be able to claim legitimate business expenses as deductions. Anything from a portion of your mortgage and maintenance payments because you turned your third bedroom into your office to the lunches and drinks and gifts you'll be doling out to round up more business will be a tax deduction.

- **Affects your retirement options.** The ability to save for retirement with an SEP or Keogh depends on the status of your business. These programs allow you to save a portion of your business income (which can be much bigger than the current maximums on Roths or traditional IRAs), let it grow tax-free, and provide you with a tax deduction.

What can you expect the lawyer and accountant to cost you? Turning yourself into a legal business can run from $500 to $1,500 or more because each state has different laws as to what you have to do to qualify for a business designation. For example, for our LLC, we had around $500 in legal preparation fees but we had to spend another $600 or so advertising in a local paper to announce the formation of our business (which is a local law). Your lawyer shouldn't have to do much more than that.

Now bring in your accountant. If you can do your own accounting as an independent contractor, wonderful. But time after time, as the *New York Times* and *Consumer Reports* have noted, it's been found that an accountant may cost more initially (from $375 to more than $2,000), but they tend to save you much more money in the long run.

There are few times when an accountant can be more helpful than when you're on your own. Keep great records of every expense; don't forget the phone bills you use for your business, subscriptions, gifts to clients, Internet usage, travel, and so on. Your accountant, who you hope has great experience with the self-employed (ask around for a personal referral), will be able to find you the deductions you need to pay what you owe and no more than that.

Setting Up Shop

You once got your pens, paper, staples, toner, business cards, and other *supplies* from your employer. Now, it's all up to you and your budget. Assess just what you'll need to set up your home shop with office supplies and get cozy with a retailer, online coupons, and coupon codes as well as comparison shopping sites to get the best prices for what you need. Your *utility costs* may also go up, depending on where you live. When you were working and commuting daily, you probably didn't use as much heat or air-conditioning as you will working at home—expect an increase of as much as 50 percent, especially for electricity usage as your computers and lights will be on now for the majority of the day.

Ah, the perks of an office phone: no extra minutes, no long-distance charges. No more. Depending on how you do business, you must review your *phone plans* to see what makes sense in terms of paying for your office phone. Is it worth using your landline? Or is your cell phone the best way for clients to reach you? Either way, shop around for the service that will best accommodate your needs and won't gouge you the second you switch from office-based chat to home office–based chat. (Watch out for Internet phone service; it may be cheap or free, but you get what you pay for. If and when the computer is down, you're down as well. A landline or extended cell phone service is best and worth the extra expense.)

You may have once done everything from holiday shop to creative corporate memos on your computer at the office, but now everything will be done on your own computer, no matter where you are. This may mean investing in a new laptop and printer for the home office. It also means secure wireless Internet service and the need for *tech support*. The costs of setting up your own office can be as little as zero if you already have everything you need or can run into the thousands if you've been working off an old dial-up desktop. These are also costs that will recoup themselves eventually. You'll run easily and efficiently on your own terms, but costs can also run high if you don't do it right. Shop around for what you need and look for great referrals for local tech support; you may be surprised by how many other freelancers and small businesses around you are also in need of a local tech guy.

> **Looking to Go Freelance?**
>
> Check out these websites:
> - Guru Employer (www.guru.com)
> - Solo Gig (www.sologig.com)
> - Elance (www.elance.com)
> - Freelancers Union (www.freelancers union.org)
> - Virtual Assistants (www.virtualassistants .com)
> - oDesk (www.odesk.com)

There is one tech business builder that may cost but nearly everyone needs: the cost of building and maintaining a *website*. If you're already established and have clients, you may think you don't need a website. But eventually some of those clients will go, and you absolutely need a website to build and market a freelance business or small business these days. Scour your friends and contacts first for high-quality but affordable site builders and designers who not only will get the site up and running but guide you through the process and teach you how to update the site yourself once it's built. Figure anywhere from $600 for the simplest design and interface to $1,000 or more for a basic site with a half dozen pages. That's just to get started. Maintenance of the site and domain registration can run $100 or more a month so factor that into your budget, as well as a tax deduction. Spending around $1,200 on the site for my first book was the best bit of marketing money I've ever spent, and it paid for itself in a whole new, lucrative career.

I've Got Stuff to Sell!

If you actually have material goods to sell, instead of a skill (writing, photography, web design, etc.), the initial costs to set up your business will be much higher. You may still be home based, but you'll need to spend more on marketing (sending out freebies, for example); you'll need to manufacture the inventory itself, which will cost in everything from materials to design to transport. There's postage and shipping, any license or permit you may need, and any advertising you'd like to do as well as any additional staff you might need to get things rolling.

It's easier to *gauge when you'll break even* when all you need is to build a website and buy some toner. But when you're looking to sell a product line as your business, rather than a service, you need to figure out when you've sold enough product to cover costs. Tally up your total fixed costs for the year (these are your utilities, rent, pay, and so on). Figure out how much it costs you to make each unit (variable cost), and subtract that number from what you're charging for each unit. Let's say you're selling makeup pencils. It costs you about $2.80 to manufacture, market, and distribute each pencil and you're going to charge $12 per pencil: $12 − $2.80 = $9.20. Now say your total fixed costs for the year come out to $10,000. Divide that by your profit per unit to find your goal: $10,000 ÷ $9.20 = 1,087. You'll need to sell over 1,000 pencils to break even, to go from a loss to a profit in your business.

This is a great reason to keep costs down as much as possible. You don't want to skimp on quality, but if you can be brave enough to negotiate better rates on necessities like design, barter with favors instead of cash payments, and lower your electricity bill, your break-even point will come sooner, and your business will go from costing you to paying you. And don't think that raising the price is always the answer. Charge a well-researched price, no more, no less—a price that is in line with the market for what you're selling. Pricier does not always mean better, and many a small business has found out the hard way that if you charge too much, someone with a lower price is more than happy to take your business. Let's say you were able to negotiate the price per pencil down on manufacturing, bringing your total variable cost per unit to

How can you **increase profit** if what you're selling are your skills? By delivering quality, keeping expenses low, building a reputation, expanding your network, and not underselling yourself.

Too many folks who start freelancing get desperate and accept extremely low pay, especially for web-based work. There's a difference between doing freebies for a big-name client that will garner you eyeballs and a great line on your résumé vs. doing work for low pay and no exposure only because you have nothing else lined up and are desperate to get business.

Keep your prices per project at the level you deserve, and if you're worried about making ends meet, it makes more sense in terms of long-term growth to take on a part-time job that pays more than to tie your name to something that has little value to your growing business and a too-tiny check.

$2.40, and you cut your fixed costs by $100 a month. You'd break even on 170 fewer pencils—that's 170 pencils of profit.

Loans

Every year around 70 percent of small business owners and freelancers use credit cards to bridge gaps in income. Until the CARD Act came into effect, little attention was paid to the fact that credit cards are not only the bane of spendaholics, but a financial tool essential for those who work for themselves. Unfortunately, as much as the CARD Act (this is the first regulation by the government of the credit card industry) helped us as credit card users, the one group of people that it has cost—in lost safety nets—is the self-employed. The CARD Act states that you must prove income to get a credit card and a corresponding credit limit. For someone starting a business with no revenue yet, this is problematic. Get your credit cards while you have predictable income so you don't fall into this rut.

Though credit cards can be a responsible tool to help take you from a first-quarter dry spell to third-quarter bonanza, leaning on credit cards too much or using them to fund your business venture can cost too much. For example, if you fund your business on credit cards (which many a fabled movie director/producer has done), know that though these are business expenses, you will be personally responsible for your credit record and for payments. This means if the business does not work out, you could be saddled, personally, with five figures or more of debt that could put any and all of your other assets in danger (except your retirement accounts; IRAs do not get drained in bankruptcy).

Nearly all initial business loans are made and backed by your personal credit and assets, but there is another reason why credit cards may not always be the way to go if you need to borrow more than, let's say, $1,000: Interest rates and terms are too expensive. Most credit cards now have variable rates and these rates average over 13 percent as I write. Fees on credit cards have gone up over 25 percent through 2010, and so far, caps on all fees and interest rates don't exist. Borrowing the $10,000 you need to start up your makeup line by plopping it all on your plastic can cost you much too much, as easy as it is compared to getting a formal business loan. Let's say it takes you a little over two years (I'm being positive here!) to pay that $10,000 back at 14 percent. You'll have to earn another $1,800+ in interest payments to get rid of that debt.

How much would you save if you went through the more rigorous application process for a Small Business Administration (SBA) loan? An SBA loan is a government-backed guaranteed loan and a federal program to help support small business owners. The good news is that because it's a federal program, there are limits on interest rates. And what determines your interest rate has to do with how big your loan is and how long you take to pay it, not only your credit history. That $10,000 would fall under the prime rate (LIBOR) plus 2.25 percent if you agree to pay it off before seven years. Prime right now is around 4.5 percent so your interest rate would be closer to 6.75 percent, less than half that of your credit card, and you'd save $1,000 in interest over two years. Need to take longer to pay back the loan? You'll still save even more going with the government rather than plastic.

The cost of SBA loans can be more about time waiting and doing paperwork. You can get an SBA loan from your local bank or credit union (which may be a better bet than a big bank). They'll usually require a business plan, projected balance sheets (how much you think you'll make in the upcoming year), projections of expenses, and cash flow and break-even estimates. Every lender is different but come prepared with a résumé as well. Some private lenders, such as credit unions, offer their own loans; make sure that you lock in a fixed interest rate that is competitive with SBA loans and credit cards. Lenders also offer SBA guaranty loans, which require approval from the lender plus approval by the SBA. Unfortunately, nabbing a great interest rate can take a lot of time. The cost of time spent waiting and processing paperwork is countered more by the interest rate of the bigger the loan you're looking for. That $1,000 you'd save on that loan of $10,000 may not be worthwhile if you need to get your business up and running quickly and you are willing to take the risks of added expense that come with a credit card. You may lose business by not being able to start up right away, so assess possible business losses with the wait time vs. the interest saved.

> Approval for an **SBA loan** depends on:
>
> • Cash flow, repayment ability.
> • Management abilities and good character.
> • Collateral and equity contribution by owner.
>
> Need more information? Visit the SBA website (www.SBA.gov).

The biggest clients of peer-to-peer (P2P) lending are small business startups. You could nab a decent interest rate borrowing from a P2P site, but if your credit is good enough to land a good rate there, try to see if a private or SBA loan would get you even better. The amount of work and time going into P2P, private, and SBA funding is similar. Interest rates differ, but with P2P, folks rarely get their loans financed 100 percent right away. It can take months to get enough people to pitch in to cover what you need, and you don't get the loan piece by piece as the money comes in; it must be fully financed to go live before you can get a loan check made out to you. The wait may be worthwhile if you're done dealing with The Man, but keep in mind that the rules on P2P loans are the same as with other private loans or credit cards. Read the fine print and don't disappoint your investors/lenders!

What About Venture Capitalists and Angel Investors?

If you're looking and thinking that big—needing more than $50,000—then do your research. Know that to attract attention it will require a lot more than a kitchen-table business plan. You'll need at least a small team in place, great contacts, and lots of room for growth and income.

Each venture capitalist, or angel, has his or her own terms. Protect yourself and your idea. Get a great lawyer.

The cost of doing business shouldn't be the loss of control and business interest in what you've created.

After credit cards, the most common way many businesses get financed is through *family and friends*. It can be wonderful to have your parents or a sibling believe in you and what you do enough to put up his or her own money to help build your business. But just because it's family or friends doesn't mean you don't need contracts or to pay interest. When it comes to personal loans. which may cost a lot less financially (lower fixed interest rate and more flexible payment terms), they can end up costly you plenty, personally.

Even for a small amount, draw up an agreement as to your terms: payback time, interest rate, and monthly payments. If it's a lot of money and your friend or family member wants in on the business profits, then you need a lawyer to step in and draw up a binding and legal document that not only makes clear the terms of the loan but outlines what rights the lender has to your business. Make sure your rights as founder and principal of the business stay intact.

Turning relationships you cherish into legal mumbo jumbo can seem cold but all that legalese will serve to protect those relationships. Expectations will be in order and on paper, leaving little room for arguments. But even a contract can't completely remove the possibility of things getting ugly down the road. What if your family member or friend wants more of the company? What if he doesn't like how you're running it and, as part owner, wants that to change? Think long and hard about the personal and professional costs of going into business with a family member or friend. Some relationships are meant to not have anything to do with money.

Real $$$ Cost of Being Your Own Boss	Real Personal Cost of Being Your Own Boss
Startup costs	Substantially more working hours
Risk of loss of startup costs plus lost wages	Fewer hours for personal use
Risk of failure of business or self-employment	Distress over loss of employer wages/benefits
Legal costs of incorporating	Increased personal stress
Borrowing costs (interest)	New limits on personal relationships (friends, family)
Sporadic income	Adjustment to new schedule and work space
Cost of providing own benefits (including retirement savings and medical, disability, dental, and vision insurance/coverage)	Possible feelings of loneliness/isolation
Possible interest paid for float loans, to cover gaps in income	

Real $$$ Benefits of Being Your Own Boss	Real Personal Benefits of Being Your Own Boss
Potentially larger income levels	Fulfillment
Upside risk of substantial success	Happiness with career choice
	Resulting improvement in psychological, emotional, mental health, and relationships
	Improved physical health

The Real Cost of
Credit Cards

*Life is very hard when no one
trusts you with a credit card.*

—Art Brut

Kim is a beautiful wisp of a thirty-something who first came to me on assignment. As a blogger for *Glamour*, her job was to finally pay attention to her money, get help, and write about it, all under the title of "Lil' Miss Fortune." But it wasn't misfortune that spelled out financial doom for Kim. She was more Lil' Miss Not Pay Attention.

My job: to help her straighten out her money and subsequently, we hoped, her life. How bad could it be? She lived with her fiancé, had a healthy freelance business, and had just turned thirty. When we met, she plopped down a few reams of paper in front of me. Sued for credit card debt twice. More than four credit card bills now in collections—and they were harassing her for their money. She didn't have a dime saved. Kim lived her life check to check and tried to ignore the ringing phone, queued with people wanting to get paid. After I wrapped my mind around the mini-mountain ahead, I asked my usual question to someone in financial trouble, "How did it get this way?" Kim looked at me with her elegant eyes and shrugged. She just didn't pay attention. No one taught her how to manage credit cards, so when she was in college and got some applications, she filled them out and used them all up. As for paying them off or even back a little, Kim just didn't pay attention—to due dates, bills, notices. And now here she was, across the table from me, anxious, but ready to do something about it.

The cost of all this debt on the life she saw before her was too much. Now that she was moving ahead at a nice clip in her career and saw a wedding and maybe family ahead, she figured it was time to face some demons. I was happy to help. Battling demons is one of my favorite pastimes.

Only a few of us have not faced down bad credit card debt at some point in our lives. I've stared it straight in the eye twice (and a half) and have won. But not without feeling the cost, both financially and personally. We all know that borrowing costs, but it's not just the interest rates and fees that steal our money. There are other culprits, and knowing just how high the cost can be beyond that 17 percent interest can keep us out of credit card debt, hopefully forever.

THE COST OF CREDIT CARD DEBT

Let's clear the air. Credit cards—and debt—are not evil in and of themselves. To be able to never borrow money is to live in the land of the already-rich, or be an always renter. At the other extreme, using other people's money (OPM) to fully finance your life is ridiculous and precarious. I wouldn't be where I am today without student loans, *some* credit card debt, and a mortgage. But of all the debts to have—student loans, mortgage, auto loan—credit card debt is the least good, meaning you usually have little to show for it. A mortgage gets you a place to live; student loans, a degree so you can earn more money; an auto loan, within reason, can get you the transportation you need to get to work and earn a living.

What do you have to show for the credit card debt you've had over your lifetime? When first starting out on my own, I purchased a solid computer to build my business. I didn't have $1,400 cash at my disposal, so I charged it. I paid it off fairly quickly and it was worth every lost penny in business gained. Credit cards can perform some very big personal functions within reason: They can be a bridge as well as a safety net. For many small business owners or for folks in between jobs and/or income, credit cards can help you keep a roof over your head by taking care of some expenses that you just don't have the cash for right now. Granted, this costs money and is potentially a slippery slope, but just like I did with my credit card debt after college to bare-bones Ikea-furnish my apartment, you pay it off and have the personal reward of a place to put your head at night. Credit cards can be mini-investments. Credit cards are used millions of times in this country to purchase something that's going to be a business or is planned on providing income— like that computer. There is a rea-

---

How to Reap Credit Card Benefits at No Cost

1. Don't carry a balance/pay in full and on time.
2. Don't use cards with fees, especially ones that penalize you for not carrying a balance or too small a balance.
3. Don't use credit cards if you do not have the discipline to follow the first rule.

If you comply with the first two rules, then:

4. Use cards for daily expenses to accumulate rewards/points.
5. Keep track of points and rewards; use them to help pay for travel and/or gifts.

---

son why entrepreneurship has boomed in the past twenty years—easy access to credit. Granted, sometimes it can be foolish to charge the filming of your sure-to-be Oscar-worthy masterpiece on your plastic, and you must be ready to take that risk and pay a very steep price, but sometimes it pays off.

However, using credit cards to finance things that don't earn you a return or are not an investment in you and your future just costs too darn much. Credit cards, if used wisely, can end up paying off instead of costing, but for many folks, using credit cards is all about living beyond your means. This is where the cost gets much too high.

Let's break down the real financial costs of using credit cards.

Interest Rates

Wow. Have the costs of carrying a balance changed, or what? (Remember, interest rates *cost* only when you carry a balance.) The average APR on a credit card was 11 percent in 2005. As I write, it's closer to 14 percent. As the recession progressed, it wasn't out of the ordinary to hear from dozens of folks a day saying that the interest rate on their credit cards went up to 29.99 percent or more, from rates as low as 7 percent! Many of these folks had done nothing wrong besides woken up on the wrong side of a credit card bill during a credit crunch. I had a card with a 7.99 percent rate go up to 17.99 percent because of the "economic climate." That's $100 more for every $1,000 owed over the year! I was thankful that I didn't carry a balance on it, but when you do, that interest rate costs—a lot.

Let's say you have a $3,000 balance on one card. You haven't been able to pay it off, though you once had an APR of only 7 percent on which you were making minimum payments of $120 a month. This worked out to a horribly unfortunate schedule of not getting you out of debt for ninety-nine months (see how credit card companies calculate minimum payments so you end up in debt the nearly maximum amount of time?) and $491 in interest. Now what if your interest rate is raised to 29.99 percent? If you still only pay the minimum, you're looking at over *seventeen years* of payments and almost *$5,000* in interest payments. Aye yi yi!

What about if you were paying $300 a month on that $3,000 balance? At 7 percent, you'd be done in less than a year and only pay $100 in interest. If your interest rate was doubled to 14 percent, that would grow to a cost of double your 7 percent interest ($209), and at 29.99 percent you'd pay $496 in interest and add on another month of payments. Wouldn't you rather have that $100? Or how about that $496? I'll take the several Benjamins.

Lost Income

How do you lose income on credit card debt? Well, that money you're paying back, plus interest, plus fees, is money that could be put to work for you. Let's go through a couple of scenarios taking not only that $3,000 balance, but the $209 in interest you'd pay over *one year* at 14 percent:

Save in a high-yield savings account earning 1.5 percent = *$3,257* (with taxes and inflation, make that $3,144)

Save in a 401(k) earning at an average of 7 percent = *$3,434* (with inflation at 3.1 percent, make that $3,330)

Invest in a taxable mutual fund earning 8 percent = *$3,402* (after taxes at 25 percent and with inflation, make that $3,299)

So if you hadn't spent that $3,000 on the credit card, but had instead put it into your IRA, you'd have $3,434 in one year instead of owing and paying out $3,209 over one year.

By owing that money, you lost $434 in potential income, not to mention peace of mind.

Fees, Fees, and More Fees

The Era of the Fee-Fest began in 2009, when credit card companies (and banks in general) decided that they needed to make more money while lending less. Looking at the multitude of products lenders had at their disposal to make money, they realized that fees were a veritable cash cow. Lenders may have made billions in credit card interest in 2009, but they also made over $13 billion in credit card fees. Used to be we were able to escape fees as it was just good customer service and a competitive edge to not charge many, if any. But after the credit crunch and with the CARD Act in effect, lenders have found the loopholes, and these loopholes are fees.

Here are some of the types of fees you can find these days on a credit card:

- Paper-statement fees (cost for receiving a statement via snail mail).
- Annual fees (once the calling card of charge cards only, like American Express, annual fees are now the norm for many card issuers).
- Low-balance fees (charged if your balance owed falls below a certain amount, say $2,300; this fee can be charged every month your balance falls below the limit).

- No-balance fees (if you pay off your balance in full each month, this fee can be yours).
- Late payment fee.
- Over-limit fee (the CARD Act says you must opt in to overlimit services).
- Balance transfer fee (usually a percentage of the balance you transfer).
- Cash-advance fee.
- Application fee (usually on secured cards or subprime cards).
- Inactivity fee (a fee for the privilege of having a card that you don't use).

I could go on . . .

Let's take that $3,000 balance again. What if you don't opt out of receiving paper statements and end up getting charged $1 a month (+$12)? The card issuer has also decided to start charging an annual fee for having the card—that's $49. Then, once your balance falls below $2,300 in month three of your pay-off plan, you get charged a low-balance fee of $9 a month, which makes you mad enough that after month five you transfer the remaining balance to another card that charges a balance transfer fee of 3 percent of the transferred amount ($18 + $45). Then, you pay late once (+$29) but you are thankful you avoid getting your interest rate raised (whew!). How much have you paid in fees in total? *$153*.

That $153 that could have been added to your $3,434 total in your 401(k) or the $3,257 in your savings account. Another set of lost savings.

The Real Deal: Emergency Funds

My advice used to be: Always pay off your credit card debt since having $1,000 in the bank while you owe $1,000 means you actually have $0 or less. But the world has changed. Now it's harder to get credit, credit costs more, and it takes longer to get a job. So save up at least a minimal emergency fund, then pay off your debt pronto. It will cost you more financially in interest and lost income, but it will pay off in security. You'll be able to pay your bills if you lose your job.

Even better, if you're carrying credit card debt and have no savings, go at your budget with a hacksaw to find ways to save money *and* make more money. You are always living a potential emergency.

Credit Score

(Note: In this section I'm referring to your FICO score, the credit score that 80 percent of lenders use.) The ripple cost effect continues on to your credit report, which is reflected in your credit score. Carry too much debt (usually more than 10 percent of your available credit), too many cards (depends on your income, other debts, and so on), pay late too many times (only once can cost), and you'll very quickly see your credit score suffer. So how does a lower credit score cost you? The most direct impact you'll see is in *your ability to borrow* (not being able to borrow can cost a little or a lot, depending on how much you need to borrow and why) and *how much it will cost you to borrow*. Let's set up a scenario.

Remember Kim? Let's pretend that she and her soon-to-be hubby had wanted to buy a home at the time we met, with outstanding collections and a dismal credit score. Let's say he had been able and willing to put up the down payment and closing costs (since she had none), but they wanted to borrow together. His credit wasn't in the best shape either though, so between his score of 660 and her score of 580, all they would qualify for would be a subprime loan—even if they put down 20 percent or more—because their scores are so low. Their averaged score would be 620, which would get them an interest rate of 6.2 percent on a mortgage of $300,000, whereas someone with a credit score of 760 could at the same time apply for a mortgage and get a rate of 4.6 percent. How much would having a bad credit score cost in this scenario?

Credit Score: 620 / $300,000 thirty-year mortgage / 6.2 percent
Monthly payments: $1,837.41
Total interest paid: $361,464.36

Credit Score: 760 / $300,000 thirty-year mortgage / 4.6 percent
Monthly payments: $1,537.93
Total interest paid: $253,657.26

THE REAL COST:
$299.48 more a month
$107,807.10 over the life of the mortgage

Pricey!

Of course, not everyone with credit card debt ends up with a credit score that low, but know that a dip of even ten or twenty points can translate into higher interest rates and higher costs when it comes time to borrow again.

The Cost of Joint Credit Cards

When and if one of you decides to go nuts with a card, you both pay. Joint cards mean joint responsibility, even if you break up and never see the other person again.

Stick to separate cards, or add an authorized user onto your card. You're still responsible in full, but it may keep peace in the house. Just know that the full cost of an authorized user's credit card behavior falls on you, not on them.

Employment Costs

Of all the costs that come with managing your credit cards badly, here is one that may pack the biggest punch because it affects your bottom line: how much money you bring home. There is no doubt that many employers look at your credit reports while they consider hiring you. Peering at credit reports—and having to ask permission to do so beforehand, by the way—is more de rigueur in fields like accounting, human resources, banking, or any job that consists of you handling sensitive information and/or keeping track of money. Insurance companies can also look at your credit reports. Credit is seen as a healthy predictor of risk and responsibility. How risky of a hire will you be? If you can't manage your own money, how can you manage someone else's? If you have so much credit card debt, maybe you'll get desperate enough to steal from the company? All fair assumptions by potential employers and for insurers as well (if your credit is crazy bad, you might be a crazy risk).

Of course, with the recession and all the job loss and financial tsunami it entailed, it's more common for employers to find wonderful job candidates with horrible credit due to too many months (or years) spent unemployed and not enough saved up. If you find yourself in this scenario, the best way to lessen the potential cost of a lost job is to be up front when asked. State clearly in a letter that you attach to your file why your credit is the way it is. Maybe you've been looking for a job for a year and you had only eight months of cash savings so you had to lean on your credit cards for some time, leaving you with high balances and a lower credit score. Being proactive and up front can help make the difference between spending another expensive month living off of plastic vs. landing that $80,000 full-time-with-benefits job.

Which Pay-Off Plan Costs Less?

There are two well-known ways to pay off your credit card debt. The first, and my favorite (and tried and true), attacks the balance with the highest interest rate first, while paying the minimums on your other cards. The second is one that costs you more money, but may make you feel better—pay off the card with the lowest balance first so you feel you accomplished something and, we hope, are fueled to continue. The first way, I'll call it Quick & Dirty, will save you the most money and get you out of debt the quickest. The second way, I'll call it Soft & So-So, will cost you more money and leave you in debt longer, but may provide a more immediate feeling of satisfaction; just know you're paying a higher financial price this way. Here's an example comparing the real $$$ cost of each plan, adding $250 each month to minimum payments:

Four Credit Cards at Various Rates (Totaling $7,743)

Balance	Interest Rate
a. $2,300	17.99 percent
b. $780	12 percent
c. $1,211	29.99 percent
d. $3,452	15.99 percent

Pay-Off Plan	Time to Pay Off	Total Interest Paid
Quick & Dirty	1 year, 4 months	$921
Soft & So-So	1 year, 5 months	$1,024

Real $$$ Winner: Quick & Dirty! (Cost of Going Soft = $103)

THE PERSONAL COST OF CREDIT CARD DEBT

Paying an extra $103 to the credit card companies to make yourself feel better is just one example of the trade-offs we make with ourselves when it comes to money and credit cards. When I was in credit card debt after college and then again after a divorce (starter marriage!), opening the mail hurt physically. I'd get sick to my stomach, tense up my shoulders, grit my teeth, and on a particularly bad day just cry over what felt like a prison. Carrying credit card debt means you can't do things you love, enjoy time with friends, spend time with family, move to a better home, or just stop eating your own bad cooking, because you're working too much to make more money to pay off debt. The pain and stress of not being able to do things and of not feeling in control of your life leads to a load of personal costs.

Too much debt = stress. We know that, some of us all too well. There is little—besides behavioral psychology applied to investing—in money/psychological research that is so well known and discussed. But why do we make ourselves pay an additional price in heightened levels of physical and psychological stress for too much credit card debt? **Because it's a threat.** Too much credit card debt can threaten to take away your quality of life, where you wake up in the morning, your ability to move ahead, freedom to enjoy yourself, and so on. Debt stress can be a chronic—low-grade or high-grade—stress that stays with you day in and day out, like a ringing in your ears or worse. But what it can do to you is not imagined or all in your head. Debt stress is real, and you can pay a real price. You can wear down your immune system and make yourself prey to cold viruses, flu, increased risk of chronic disease like diabetes, and even limit or thwart your body's ability to take care of itself and heal, leading to chronic pain, anxiety, panic attacks, ulcers, teeth grinding, and more.

Just before the recession hit us hard, the Associated Press (AP) and AOL conducted a debt stress poll. The results were eye-opening, especially in light of the fact that things were about to get worse. Ten to sixteen million people reported that they were suffering terribly due to debt, and their health was negatively impacted. About 44 percent of these debt-laden folks reported migraines or other headaches, and 29 percent suffered from anxiety, 23 percent from depression, and 27 percent had ulcers or other digestive problems. Interestingly enough upwardly mobile middle-class families had the most debt stress. And in another AP poll for the holidays of 2009, 20 percent of Americans said they were suffering from debt-related stress.

Debt stress is so well known and documented now that we have a Consumer Debt Stress Index (DSI) from Ohio State University, which "measures psychological stress on consumers from all sources of debt." If you peek at the trail our DSI has run just over the past couple of years, our debt stress has followed the collapse and attempted recovery of the nation's economy. The DSI hit its low (90.3) in May 2007, just before the housing market collapsed (which illustrates also how wrapped up our psychological health is with the state of our homes and home values, as discussed in the first chapter). Then the DSI spiked to a record 155.3 in July 2009, when the you-know-what really hit the fan. And by the way, illustrating how women are too hard on ourselves, in the DSI, even at the same debt and income levels, women experienced a third more debt stress than men.

Lessen Psychological Costs

Remember how far under Kim had fallen? But as we sat down and reviewed just how much she owed and to whom, she started to feel better. **Knowledge is key.** After all, these are just numbers, right? That's how you need to think of them—numbers. Basic fourth-grade math. Avoidance gives you only the illusion of control and relief. Actually, when you don't know how much you owe or just how bad it's getting, your mind can make up a new reality, and sometimes the *real* reality is better than what you've made up in your head. Consider it a swift form of exposure therapy. Let's say you're scared of spiders.

There's lots of data out there that show that if you expose yourself to spiders on a regular basis, your fear and anxiety goes away. Go ahead. Touch that spider. Open that credit card bill!

Once you know exactly how much you owe on each card and your APRs and fees, it's time for Mach 2: **Put a plan in action.** Tackle those credit cards, preferably the Quick & Dirty way.

We had a segment on the show that took folks in credit card debt and showed them just how quickly they could get out if they followed my Quick & Dirty formula and put more money toward the debt every month. The cries, sighs, laughs of relief when I showed people how another $100 or $200 a month could save them thousands of dollars and *years* of debt stress were some of the best rewards of my career. Try it yourself. Punch your numbers in the financial calculator at www.dinkytown.net, choose "Pay card with highest interest rate first," and see just what another $100 or even just $50 a month can do. This is all part of putting your plan into action. *It puts you in control.* Feeling in control always works to neutralize, a bit or a lot, a perceived threat.

Still feeling like it's too much? *Get help.* Enlist family, friends, or in the worst-case scenarios a nonprofit credit counselor (find one from National Foundation for Credit Counseling at www.nfcc.org). Some battles we should not fight alone. Plus, you need your friends on your side to help you control your spending; dump or avoid any friend that turns frenemy on you here (by bullying you into going out or making you feel bad for staying in and not spending). They cost you too much, personally and financially.

Real $$$ Cost of Credit Card Debt	Real Personal Cost of Credit Card Debt
Interest payments	Stress, anxiety, depression
Fees	Exacerbates other physical/psychological problems/symptoms (ulcers, diabetes, chronic illness)
Credit score/higher interest on other loans	Perception of no control, loss of freedom, being trapped
Potential employment/insurance repercussions	
Limited means to pursue other goals	

Real $$$ Benefits of No Credit Card Debt	Real Personal Benefits of No Credit Card Debt
Additional funds to save, invest, or pursue other goals	Lower stress and anxiety levels; better health overall
Better credit scores, better rates on other loans	More physical/psychological energy to spend on fruitful endeavors
Better insurance and employment rates	Feeling of freedom, independence, control

THE COST OF *NOT* HAVING CREDIT CARDS

I had just wrapped up a lecture to a roomful of college students and was chatting with friendly stragglers afterward when one rather put-together hipster approached me to proclaim with great pride: "I don't have *any* credit cards and I don't plan on ever getting one!" He seemed so well intentioned, I tread gently. There is a cost to not having credit cards. Remember, they are not evil in and of themselves. **Credit cards are merely a tool in our personal finance portfolio of life.** They serve a purpose, whether it's as emergency-only backup or to rack up points or to float us between gigs or even to start a business. They also can protect your purchases, aid you in making purchases, get you free rewards, and build credit. Not having credit cards at all carries *a cost that is all about losing benefits.*

Purchase Protection

Most credit cards offer a kind of insurance on what you buy with them called purchase protection. Usually you have ninety days to file a claim for a supposedly good deal gone bad, let's say a lemon of a computer you bought online or maybe you didn't even receive the item at all or it was stolen. Ensuring that what you buy can be replaced if it's lost, damaged, fraudulent, or stolen is a nice perk of credit cards. And it's not cash out of your pocket, as with a debit card (see what follows for more on debit dangers). This is an excellent reason why you should always use a credit card when you shop online and when you travel. But be careful: Some purchase protection programs have some very strange loopholes, such as limiting protection to purchases within a certain geographical distance from you or a certain dollar amount. Know which of your cards has the best policy, make sure you have the cash to pay the bill in full, and use that one.

Travel Freedom and Insurance

If that spritely hipster had tried to rent a car—after he turned twenty-five, of course—without a credit card, he may be in for a surprise.

Renting a car requires a card of some sort, and using a debit card to book a rental car is very, very unwise (see later for debit dangers) and sometimes just not possible. Can you imagine trying to book and pay for a family vacation all in cash? You certainly couldn't book it online and possibly save hundreds of dollars (costly!) and you'd also be out of any type of protection or coverage should something go wrong. There is little doubt that credit cards have given us a world of travel and an ability to go from country to country without fear of running out of euros, pesos, dollars, or pounds. Charging your travel on a credit card with good terms can also give you valuable insurance coverage that greatly outweighs your desire to never have plastic, or in my case an annual fee.

For example, my husband and I recently put our family mini-vacation on our gold American Express. I made sure before booking to review what kind of travel coverage the card had—and it was good. So good in fact that the $49 annual fee paid for itself several times over when the rental Jeep bumped into a tree, smashing a taillight. (Oops.) Some phone calls and two bits of paperwork, and the card covered all the damage, around $400. Another advantage of having good credit is you get access to better cards with better perks. If you travel often, using a credit card with additional baggage, flight, cancellation, rental car, and even medical and life insurance can lower the costs of travel significantly. Your credit card functions as additional insurance.

Trouble Getting a Credit Card?

Try a **secured card** (*not* a prepaid card). A secured card has you plop down a certain amount of cash, say $300, onto the card. You then use the card as you would a debit. You keep replenishing the card with cash as you use it. After a year or two of good behavior, you'll be extended credit.

Make sure the secured card you go with reports to the credit bureaus so you can build up your credit score.

Shop at Bankrate (www.bankrate.com) or Credit.com (www.credit.com) for a secured card.

Rewards/Points

There live in some parts of the land people known as "point junkies." They cost credit card companies *a lot*, and some even say that they cost regular card users as lenders trickle down the cost of subsidizing their rewards with higher rates for everyone else. Point junkies charge absolutely everything (when I worked at Christie's auction house right out of college, there was a client who wanted to pay for his $1.5 million painting with his American Express to rack up points!) so they can use points and rewards to travel or buy gifts or pretty much anything. Then there are folks like me who charge household spending on a reward card to pile up just enough points to buy gifts or get visiting family a nice hotel room once in a while. There is no doubt that I've saved hundreds of dollars in necessary purchases via rewards, all while *not* carrying a balance. Rewards and points mean almost nothing if you're paying interest. And rewards and points policies can change; it's a perk that can potentially be taken away, so make sure to read the fine print. If you'd rather get your rewards in cold, hard cash, go with cash-back cards. (Why do I stick with my reward card? Because it also carries incredible insurance I haven't been able to match with a cash-back card, though I'm waiting!) Cards with rewards, points, and cash back tend to go to only those with very good credit and some have hidden, costly terms such as too-high annual fees, high interest rates, or other fees. So, shop around, shop wisely, and avoid carrying a balance, or else there's no point. Heh.

Build Credit

When my plastic-free college buddy goes to rent an apartment, what will his potential landlord see on his credit report? Maybe a student loan. But a student loan plus a credit card managed well would probably be better. And what about when he applies for an auto loan? Varied forms of credit can raise your credit score and populate your credit report with enough good news to get you that apartment or that low-interest auto loan. A portion of how your credit score is calculated depends on the different types of loans or lines of credit you're carrying. Consider disciplined use of credit cards another part of your credit portfolio, and as I wrote earlier, good credit means borrowing, even living, costs less.

Real $$$ Cost of Not Having Credit Cards	Real Personal Cost of Not Having Credit Cards
Potentially lower credit scores, higher rates on other loans	Distress over inability to travel freely or purchase certain items
Inability to save money on travel and insurance	Concern over losses to theft, fraud
Inability to travel, rent cars, purchase certain items	Perception of limited resources in case of emergency (What happens if . . . ?)
Loss of purchase protection in case of fraud, theft, damaged goods	Lower credit score can limit freedom to live, work where you most want to
Limited resources in case of emergency	

Real $$$ Benefits of Having Credit Cards	Real Personal Benefits of Having Credit Cards
Emergency resource	Lessened anxiety (emergency resource at hand; perception of freedom to travel with assurance of added insurance, guarantees, purchase protection, potentially better credit scores)
Freedom to travel (book hotels, flights, car rentals at the best prices)	
Additional insurance and travel coverage	
Rewards, points, cash back	
Purchase protection	
Potentially better credit scores	

EXTRA CREDIT: THE REAL COST OF DEBIT CARDS

Debit cards are the (unfortunate) wave of the future. By 2012, debit cards will outpace cash as the number one way we pay for things. Debit cards have outpaced credit cards already. For this, I mourn. Why? Because debit cards contributed to the banking industry making $27 billion in overdraft fees in 2009. My dislike of debit cards is the one topic that wins me the most ire. How dare I recommend credit cards over debit cards?! I must be advocating debt and, therefore, I am evil and immoral! Well, the nuns who schooled me can surely attest that I am not evil (though sometimes rebellious). So how can so much of America be so wrong? Why do I dislike debit cards so much? *Because they cost too much.*

Plastic is a business. Debit cards are plastic; therefore, they are a business. Banks see how much we're using our debit cards, and as I write, they are unregulated, unlike credit cards. Therefore, ka-ching! What a great way to raise bank revenue. Between overdraft fees (multiple fees in one day, not to mention one month, are more common than you think), bounced check fees, lost cash due to a mix-up at the register or theft, hacked cards that clean out bank accounts . . . debit cards *cost*.

Maybe they don't cost you . . . yet. Maybe you always keep a nice cushion in your checking account and review your statements regularly and note every purchase. But what if you're like *The Case of the $2,000 T-Shirt*? A gentleman we'll call Roger contacted the show for a debit card segment I was geared up to do. I couldn't have made up this debit card drama. Roger had been on vacation with his wife in

Jamaica and saw a wonderful, sparkly, tie-dyed T-shirt he wanted to buy her as a surprise gift. So, he bought it . . . using his debit card. Now, was this T-shirt really $2,000? Nope. The tag said $2,000 *Jamaican*. But the person at the register entered $2,000US, emptying Roger's checking account, leaving no funds for bills he had paid or other cash. Roger came on the show, and we had an amazing response. His bank at first agreed with him and refunded the money, but then they reneged and took the money back! Final verdict: The bank said that he signed a receipt that said $2,000US; therefore, he was liable for the full amount. Roger's very costly mistake was that he didn't see a very faint "U.S." on the receipt he was signing. But had he used a credit card, the funds would have been in dispute, not cash out of his pocket. And he would have been much more likely to pay what he really wanted to agree to, $35US.

Debit cards are tied to your cash. If you make a mistaken purchase, if a cashier rings you up wrong, if a hacker hacks into your account, your cash is gone. Granted, you should get it back after you contact the bank and make the right moves, but in that time the cash is gone, many things can happen. You can bounce a rent check or be late with a mortgage or credit card payment that didn't go through, stealing points from your credit score. You can be without cash when you need it, necessitating borrowing from someone or taking out a cash advance, which costs. Why risk it?

Also, don't think that only lazy, undisciplined people overdraw their accounts. If you use your debit card to rent a car, you can be out a lot more than the agreed-upon $49 a day. Rental companies must reserve room on your card just in case something goes wrong, so you can see $500 disappear into their reserve, and checks can bounce in the meantime. Also, if you use your debit card at the gas station, some stations reserve $100 off of your account just in case you fill up and run.

But should everyone avoid debit cards? Not really. Definitely not if you are one of the 20 percent or less of Americans who tend to get into credit card debt. If using a credit card instead of a debit card means that you'll overspend or you'll let your payments slide—because you know you can—then you need to make a choice and an acknowledgment: that you realize there are risks to using debit, but that cost is worthwhile to you because you know you'll end up paying more using a credit card and potentially carrying a balance. However, you should always choose a credit card with purchase protection and hopefully additional travel insurance when you book travel. Do your best to not go over budget.

How to Lessen the Cost If You Can't Pay

Not paying your credit card bills should not be an option unless you're on your last money legs, and even then, always keep the lines of communication open between you and the credit card company. If you find that you can't pay your bill, even a newly negotiated lower bill, there are some steps you can take to lessen the cost of dropping—or having to drop—this ball. And remember, if you need help along the way with any of these steps, find a nonprofit credit counselor to work with you from the National Foundation for Credit Counseling (www.nfcc.org).

First, *try to settle*. If you are unable to pay your monthly credit card bill, but you could get your hands on a lump of cash from someone or somewhere, you can try to negotiate a settlement with your credit card company. They don't like to do it and surely don't advertise that it's a possibility, but it can be done. What a settlement does is enter you into a new agreement for the debt, based on the total amount you both agree on to pay. Let's say you owe a total of $15,000 on a credit card but you've been out of work for too long and just can't make the minimum payments. But you know you could find $10,000 to pay a lump sum of it. You call the credit card company, ask for a manager or supervisor (of course), and try to negotiate a settlement for a lump sum payment of $10,000. Now, you may not get it, but here's what increases your odds: if you don't have any assets. This is very important. Credit card companies do not, for the most part, want to negotiate settlements with someone who has assets of value, like a home or investments (outside of IRAs). If you have assets, that means you can sell stuff to pay your balance; therefore, their odds of getting all their money back are better. But if you're a renter and have no assets that they can go after, some credit card companies may be willing to settle for less than you owe. Your credit will take a hit, of course. And I don't recommend this for anyone but those in the most dire circumstances, because outside of medical bills (which you shouldn't put on a credit card anyway), if you have credit card debt, you should pay it back—all of it. Unless it's already in collections.

Once your credit card debt, or another debt, has gone into collections, it ceases or barely exists. *Collection companies* buy your credit card debt from the lender for ten or twelve cents on the dollar. To the credit card company, your debt

If you're being harassed by bill collectors—and they can be a nasty bunch—first, know that you have rights.

Next time they call say, "I have rights according to the Fair Debt Collection Practices Act, and I expect you to respect those rights." You'd be surprised in their change in tone.

Arm yourself with your rights which you can find at the Federal Trade Commission's website (www.ftc.gov); click on "Quick Finder: Debt Collection."

is gone; it's been wiped from their books. The collection agency's job is to get a portion of it back (that ten to twelve cents on the dollar) and make a profit off the rest that you pay. So if you owe $15,000 and pay back that amount to a collection agency, they're looking at a juicy profit. This little secret is why you should always try to negotiate down a collections balance.

A little less than six months after I first sat down with Kim, she had followed my advice and came back on the show to take us through just how far she had come. Remember those items she had had in collections? Well, armed with some knowledge, my pep talks and scripts, and her perky charm, Kim had managed to take her total collections balance down by $14,000. Fourteen *thousand* dollars! That was around a third of what she had owed in total. Just by knowing that she could, being brave, and using the phone, Kim had saved herself five figures. Now, some of you will say, "Wait! She spent it, she owes it—in full!" Remember, it was in collections. Her initial debt was gone, wiped out when the collection agency bought it from the credit card company. She didn't owe the credit card company anymore; she owed the collection agency. The only reason I encourage folks to talk down collections is that paying a collection company nearly 80 percent profit is not a cost you need to bear. Be nice, know your rights, and save some money. (Now is this a question of ethics? After all, if you run up the debt and spend the money, aren't you obligated to pay it back? It may depend on how and why you accumulated the debt, but in the end, accounting, ethics, and collections point in different directions, and it's up to you to make the call and decide on your final cost.)

What about if you *get sued*? Kim had also been sued (twice!) for not paying her credit card bills. This is something you want to avoid as much as possible. Once you've been sued, what you owe is locked in—no collections, no negotiating—and you may have to spend money on your own lawyer. This is the most costly end of the can't-pay stick. When you don't pay your credit card bills, the odds are that it will go to collections since suing you costs money. But sometimes the credit card company can afford to sue you, and they feel like their chances are good for getting their money back. Kim paid back both balances that she was sued for, in full, and then some (penalties, legal fees, etc.).

The damage to your credit is the highest cost you may pay for not paying credit card debt. Sure, there will be penalties, late fees, interest, and so on that will cost a sometimes ridiculous amount compared to what you initially owed. But all these costs can be paid off, sometimes much more quickly than your credit score and reports can recover. But when life really throws you a hard one, bankruptcy may be the answer.

The Real Deal: Bankruptcy

Chapter 13
A repayment plan. Mostly for folks who can earn enough to repay debts over a three- to five-year basis; payment schedules and amounts are determined by the court.

Chapter 7
Liquidation of assets (though, depending on the state, your home, car, and other assets may be exempt). Quick and easy but you must pass a means test to even apply. Many don't pass and end up with Chapter 13.

What's the Cost of Bankruptcy?

The cost of bankruptcy is your credit in the toilet and a lot of drama. You may not be able to get a mortgage for two to three years, maybe five years if you're looking for a competitive interest rate. It will be very hard to find a landlord willing to rent to you and even harder to build your credit back up, get credit cards, maybe even get a job (discussed earlier in the chapter). Bankruptcy devastates lives and families, and surely, there are many who still feel its sting of humiliation. (Despite the grumblings of some politicians who say Americans are filing willy-nilly because it no longer carries a stigma. Hogwash.) But if you must look at bankruptcy, be embarrassed only if you got yourself there for selfish reasons, and in that case, learn from it. If you're in that situation out of little or no doing of your own—medical bills, disability, caring for a sick child or parent, for example—it may be a good thing, and the financial cost of damaged credit and hours with a lawyer may all be worth it for the personal benefit of moving forward and starting over.

Michelle was a lovely blond mom from Nevada who contacted me because she was loaded with debt and just didn't know what to do. She was working three jobs to pay her bills and credit card debt because her sixteen-year-old daughter had been diagnosed with cancer and her care cost a fortune. Michelle was terrified of bankruptcy and wanted to do the right thing and pay her bills. But I told her the opposite. The right thing was to quit her jobs (at least two of them) the *next day* and spend valuable, precious, priceless time with her daughter who may or may not be around for much longer. I told her to file bankruptcy as soon as possible. Lovely Michelle and her daughter were paying too high a price for all that debt—debt that came on them only because a child had the bad luck of falling ill without great health insurance. An extreme situation, yes. But when you think about the cost of should I or shouldn't I with bankruptcy, ask what's at stake and why.

HOW TO LOWER THE COST OF CREDIT CARDS

If you must carry a balance on your credit cards, this is how you lower the cost:

- **Get out as soon as possible.** Remember the Quick & Easy example? What if I had lowered that pay-off plan from $250 to $200 a month in addition to the minimum payment? That would cost me an additional $115 in interest and two more months. The sooner you can get rid of your balance, the better and less costly—always!
- **Maintain a high credit score.** Higher credit scores translate into lower interest rates, but not always, as the Land of Credit has become the Wild Wild West. Higher scores also give you the freedom to do the next two steps.
- **Surf your balance.** If you have a balance with a card that has a high interest rate while you have another card with a much lower interest rate, you can surf the balance over to your lower-rate card. Pay attention, however, to how much the balance transfer will cost you. In the days of 0 percent rates for twelve months or more, it didn't matter, but if the difference in interest between the cards isn't that much, the transfer cost may be too

pricey. It also depends on how long you plan on carrying the balance; the longer you have it, the more the transfer will usually make sense. Calculate your balance transfer fee and plug in your balance at the two different interest rates in one of the financial calculators at Dinkytown.net.

- **Open another card with a lower balance.** There's that good credit score again: If you have one, you can open another credit card and surf your balance to a card with a lower rate. Shop around, hard, for cards at sites like Bankrate (www.bankrate .com) and LowCard\$ (www.lowcards.com). Just remember, advertised rates are not necessarily the rates you'll get unless you have sparkling credit (at or above 760).

Let's check in on Kim. Eight months after I met with her, she had been transferred to another assignment: blogging about her upcoming wedding. Why? Because she was no longer Lil' Miss Fortune! Kim had managed to dig herself out of what was originally around \$60,000 of debt and she'd even saved up some cash, put more money into her retirement accounts, and in celebration, bought herself a \$450 purse.

But that's another story.

Real \$\$\$ Cost of Bankruptcy	Real Personal Cost of Bankruptcy
Possible liquidation and loss of assets, including home and savings	Distress over legal proceedings
Severely damaged credit record and credit score	Distress over loss of assets

Real $$$ Cost of Bankruptcy	Real Personal Cost of Bankruptcy
Inability to borrow for several years, and when able, only at very high prices	Embarrassment, humiliation, feelings of failure
Possible loss of job opportunity (if job requires credit check)	Adjustment of family life if move is necessary
	Distress over limited abilities to spend, adjust lifestyle (especially if includes court monitoring of budget)
	Possible loss of job opportunities and advancement in career

Real $$$ Benefits of Bankruptcy	Real Personal Benefits of Bankruptcy
Assessment and review of debts and family budget, retooled by judge (Chapter 13)	End to possible overworking while trying to pay all debts (less distress over unmanageable debts)
Preservation of home, car, and IRA funds (especially Chapter 13)	End to potentially harassing debt collectors
Enrollment in court-monitored debt repayment plan (Chapter 13)	Relief over final judgment made on assets, home
Ability to start fresh and rebuild credit, finances	Hope in regard to ability to rebuild credit, start over

The Real Cost of
Saving

*If we expect others to pay us, we
shouldn't expect less from ourselves.*

S teve was a swell guy. A bubbly baby boomer from Staten Island,
Steve had come to me for advice months earlier, anguished about
the state of his money. But on that morning, all we heard was joy.

"Carmen, you *have* to hear this! It's Steve from Staten Island!"
Dawn, one of my favorite producers (who I fittingly called "Sun-
shine"), read emails from viewers and listened to voicemail to see
who could use the most help on the show. Today, Steve's voicemail
had her greeting me with an infectious laugh. With his gravelly voice
and distinct accent, Steve from Staten Island asked Dawn to thank
me so much for my advice. He had been following it for two months
now, and he and his wife not only paid off debt and started saving
money, but he had also lost twelve pounds.

Steve had had a very common problem, especially at that time
right before the recession hit us all big. He and his wife were in their

fifties yet they had barely any cash savings at all. They just didn't know why. On air, as a couple (his wife smiling sweetly and supportive, though I could see the strain in her eyes and forehead), Steve said that they made decent money and had retirement savings that were taken out of their checks every month, but they just couldn't save cash. What they brought home they spent.

When someone was being considered for an appearance on the show, I required that they fill out a very detailed form: how much was coming in, where it was going out, how much was going out, along with how much they owed. I inspected Steve's finances, and I discovered a very expensive culprit: their grocery bill! Now, I like my fancy cheeses and meats but how two people could spend $650 or more a month on groceries and not see that there was room to cut, I had no idea.

I revealed the answer to their savings needs to Steve on the show: "Steve, what about this grocery bill?" That was their savings meal ticket as nearly all their other spending and debts were actually in line with where they should be. Steve was surprised but accepted the news, vowing to knock down that monthly bill. Little did he know that a recession was coming and all our savings accounts would be tested for more than two years. Saving cash money in America would never be the same.

Two months later, Steve and his wife had hundreds of dollars in a savings account which they planned on keeping up, as well as smaller waists. Steve was thrilled that he'd lost a dozen pounds (and counting) and now had the benefit of the security of savings. And getting healthy will save him more money down the road in healthcare costs (see the chapter on bad habits).

SPENDING

It's nearly impossible to talk about saving money without talking about spending it. After all, that's why money exists. We need to pay for things in life, everything from essentials to Bendy Bandz. And with all the talk about how we Americans are horrible savers, there is little talk as to why, beyond the idea that we all live above our means. Well, are we all just greedy, consumptive ogres looking for the next best Wii? Not really. What we are is struggling against a tide of pressure on our discretionary spending. This is the money we are supposed to have left over after we pay for essentials, such as our rent or mortgage, utilities, food, clothing, and such. But our wages have barely gone up (except for the top 20 percent of Americans, for whom it's gone up two hundred times, compared to the bottom 20 percent, who saw a growth of only fourteen times), while our fixed costs for essentials have practically skyrocketed. Consider that in the 1970s, nearly one-half of all our income was free to spend as we wish—it was discretionary. After food, clothing, rent or mortgage, and utilities, we had nearly 50 percent of our income left over. (Can you imagine?) There was plenty of room to spend as well as save money. Around 2004 or 2005, our income had gone up substantially but our discretionary income shrank to around 24 percent of our money. Whatever more we make goes to paying fixed costs as opposed to more spending money. So it's harder to save when you have less to save with; after all, that discretionary income has to be split somehow between spending and saving.

And spending for us isn't always about getting the best deal. I'll pay more for a brand-name face wash than I will for over-the-counter meds, which I usually buy generic. If our savings must come from the same pool as our spending money, why not shrink the spending to increase the savings?

As a kid I used to spend hours upon hours on Sundays helping my mom clip coupons from the Sunday paper and then organize them and plan the grocery list. Added bonus: There was a grocery store nearby that would double your coupons. So the whole family (six kids!) would head to that store and spend another couple of hours shopping for the week. My dad would boast at the cash register about how much we had saved; sometimes we had saved much more than we'd spent. It was pricey to support six kids on one income, and my parents' frugal ways surely paid off. But have I continued in that tradition? Even when I was barely scraping by? Nope. Even when all I could afford for dinner was a $1.50 wonton soup, I did not use grocery store or drugstore coupons. My issue with coupons has to do with time cost. I resent the amount of time spent to get toothpaste half off. I understood the pressure on a tight budget, but I was willing to eat (brand-name) cold cereal and wonton soup for a month rather than spend my valuable free time (Sunday mornings) clipping coupons. Spending and saving is not all about dollars and cents but about the real cost of saving those dollars. To me, the time cost outweighs the savings, but then again, I don't have six kids.

I was getting my makeup and hair done for a morning show when my friend and makeup artist, Janet, bubbled over telling me the amazing deal she had gotten the day before on a designer dress.

"Carmen, you *have* to see the receipt: sixty percent off, *then* another twenty percent off *and* another ten percent off because I used my store card!" I have to say, I was very impressed. Then I became mesmerized by the receipt, which showed a total of 90 percent off a dress that had an original retail price of over $1,000! Now that's what I call savvy shopping.

I may not be a coupon clipper, but you can be darn sure that I don't pay retail for barely anything outside of the grocery store, drugstore, and maybe wine store. I share Janet's need to go for the sale—to get the best quality for the absolute lowest price has become de rigueur, aided by price comparison sites, Facebook pages for retailers, promo codes, Craigslist, eBay, and Etsy. Time with scissors spent scouring over flyers is no longer a requirement to saving money when we spend. That cost has gone down, and with it our tolerance for retail pricing; sometimes even when discretionary income grows, the need to save off of retail remains. A good, helpful habit.

But it's still hard to save because we don't always want to save. We want what we want, even if it costs more or we have to pay retail because so many people want it. Take cars, for example. Why does my family insist on buying brand-new cars, especially sometimes on limited budgets, when they could have a better car for the same price (or less) by just buying used or certified preowned (CPO)? Many of us just will not buy a used car, even if it means getting more car for your buck. After all, you lose thousands to depreciation the second you drive a new car off the lot. Something that doesn't happen when you buy a car with some miles on it. Sales of CPO vehicles went up substantially due to the recession but they are still not even close to the sale of new cars. There's a stigma attached. A stigma and a desire for new that costs us thousands that instead could be saved or could be put into a safer, better car that will last longer. Our personal desires and needs can way outweigh our desire to save. We love brands, and we're attached to certain ideals of purchase: a new car vs. one with a thousand miles on it, for example. And we pay a price for that, even more pressure on our dwindling discretionary income. That price can sometimes become unaffordable.

THE REAL COST OF NOT SAVING CASH

When's the last time you went to the circus? Most of us went when we were kids but then didn't go again until eons later, when we had kids of our own. Count me in. My husband and I took our daughter to the Big Apple Circus for her third birthday—my first circus jaunt in over two decades. There were rings tossed, things juggled, and clowns (which I don't like). But my favorite has always been the trapeze. This one was small and fun and, I was happy to see, had a nice, big safety net. Some circuses pride themselves on having a trapeze act without a safety net, to add to the level of excitement. That's not excitement to me—it's dread. No, I do not want to see a human being splattered on the circus floor, and no, the possibility of that happening does not thrill me in the slightest. I'm a fan of safety nets, not snuff.

That's exactly what our cash savings should function as: a safety net when we fall, financially and even personally. With the Great Recession, what we found out quickly and dramatically, together as a nation, was that not having a safety net in the form of cash savings is a very expensive and dramatic mistake.

So how much did it cost as a country to not have that cash net, ready to help when jobs went away? The price tag of extending unemployment benefits to millions of Americans as part of the stimulus package ran us about $100 billion. Despite this, 5.1 million of us foreclosed on our property in two years (2008 to 2009), pulling down the value of all our homes and resulting in a loss of $500 billion in home value and disappearing equity. Personal bankruptcies went up 32 percent to 1.41 million Americans. The cost of not continuing the once-valued tradition of saving a chunk of the money we make has cost us all, dearly and possibly for decades.

But what does it look like to an individual or family to not have saved enough money to cover six to eight months of living expenses? What could be the real financial cost of not saving? First, let's address living expenses. Why do we say six to eight months of living expenses vs. six to eight months of pay? Because in dire times, you need to go into survival mode—winter mode. You can't and shouldn't function as if nothing were wrong or different when something does go wrong and is different. I call it lock-down. Picture yourself in a bunker. You've only got so much to live on and a period of time to do it, so it's time to ration. You need to spend money on only what's essential, your living expenses. What makes it into the category of living expenses may differ a bit from person to person and is subject to different comfort levels (Will you croak without cable? Or will you tithe, no matter how low your money goes?), but there are a couple of items we can all agree on:

- Monthly housing expenses (what you spend on your mortgage payment, home insurance, property taxes, maintenance fees, and/or rent every month).
- Food (not restaurant food, but bare-bones eat-at-home-and-use-coupons food).
- Heat, hot water, electricity.
- Transportation (keeping it to as needed vs. I feel like a road trip).

Many of us would add medical, dental, life, and/or disability coverage; childcare and/or schooling; and other essentials, such as prescriptions, student loans, and other debt obligations.

If you haven't already, add up how much your essential living expenses total each month and compare that to how much you take home every month. You may be surprised to see either a very small gap in between or pleased by a very big one. It's a good exercise to see just how much you need to keep a decent quality of life when things get rough.

We know what the financial cost of not saving looks like: a potentially ugly scene and years of clawing your way back into the green. But just how much of a toll does it take on you personally? There are few things you'll do in life with your money that could cost as much as not saving.

At the extreme, how much anguish would losing your home cause you? Your pride, self-worth, and potential to move forward professionally and personally is damaged. If you already have anxiety disorders, it gets worse. Depression, risky behavior, drinking too much . . . all can result from the stress of losing your home or seeing the potential of losing your home looming.

A report published in *USA Today* as the foreclosure crisis went into full swing stated that psychological crisis hotlines were lighting up with folks in fear of losing their homes. The American Psychological Association's website listed tips on how to deal with the housing crisis. The news was full of stories of suicides by people who were losing their homes. And what about the children who have to move, changing schools, losing friends, and adjusting to new routines? The cost for them is higher, though they have more time to recover. Now, I am not trying to scare you straight so you save. Well, maybe I am. And even in the best scenarios when you have some savings and just eke by, that eking is stressful.

But it can also cost you personally to put away money for a rainy day. For example, when you have to save money, you can't spend it. It can hurt to not be able to go out to dinner or take the kids on vacation this year or sacrifice your biweekly manicures to save up the emergency fund you need so much. There is no doubt that saving money instead of spending money has an immediate opportunity cost. It costs you personally to not have the immediate satisfaction of that money at your fingertips to do what you want with it. This can be why it is so hard for many of us to save. We'd rather have the money now to do what we want with it. Or we feel that our budgets are too tight to squeeze any more. It will hurt (cost) too much to save.

SAVING MONEY COSTS MONEY

It costs to save? Did I not just talk about how costly it is to not save? How does saving money cost? Well, in the days of 1.5 percent interest rates on savings and money market accounts, saving money costs money. Here's why.

It's the one form of family savings where there is *no tax advantage.* We have tax-friendly retirement savings options and tax-friendly education savings accounts, but for plain old personal savings—in case of emergency, for a family vacation, for a down payment on a home—we don't get a tax break to encourage us to save cash. So come April 15, we all get a statement showing how much interest we earned on our personal bank accounts (I once got one when I was in my twenties for $.86), and we must declare those earnings to the IRS as income. So those tiny interest earnings get cut down further (how far depends on your tax bracket).

On a purely monetary argument, it actually doesn't make immediate financial sense to have a savings account without tax advantages. When I hear from folks without cash savings accounts, they almost all have retirement savings accounts, which are an employee benefit, and the funds are taken out of their paychecks before they even see them, locking them up in essence so the money can grow tax-free.

> **Mini-Rant**
>
> Interest earned from personal savings accounts* should *not* be taxed!
>
> *Accounts not to exceed a ceiling of, say, $100,000 cash savings per household to discourage the top 1 percent of earners from creating another tax loophole.

There's another little monster that eats away at our savings accounts, shrinking our dollars little by little, bolstering the argument for the need for some tax relief: *inflation*. Think of inflation as your dollar's buying power shrinking. So one year you have $1 but because the costs of goods and expenses rose 3 percent over the course of that year, the following year, your buying power with that dollar has shrunken to essentially $.97. Imagine the tug and pull your cash savings undergo over time as inflation plus taxes eat away at what you're putting away:

Let's say you have a savings account with $10,000 in it. The rate of inflation that year is 3 percent. So by the next year your savings are an adjusted $9,700 (though your statement says you haven't lost a dime, your buying power has decreased $300). You were smart enough to find an interest-bearing savings account that gets you 1.5

percent in interest, so after one year you have $150 in your account to counter that inflation hit of $300. (Yay! $150 closer to having what you put in there in the first place.) But then . . . the taxman cometh and you are taxed on those earnings of $150 on your savings, bringing you back down to more like $90 on your $10,000 after one year. Add in inflation and your savings account is less $210. And we could all use another $210 a year.

It wasn't always this way. Back in the rah-rah-boom days, you could get 3.5 percent interest easily on your savings account. Our savings, money market accounts, and CD rates are tied to the Federal Reserve rate, which is set by the government. As I write, and for a long time now, the rate has been set at nearly 0 percent. When the federal interest rate is low, interest earned on cash savings is low, but borrowing rates are supposed to be low, too. (These rules were sometimes pushed and pulled out of joint in the Great Recession because there are so many other factors weighing in on the decision of what interest rate to offer, such as the credit crunch and the CARD Act, which prompted lenders to give us sky-high interest rates on our credit cards.) When the federal rate is higher, and we're not in a recession, the interest we can earn on our accounts is higher, as are our borrowing rates for things like mortgages. So before the recession, we saw rates like 3.5 percent on savings accounts, even 5 percent on CDs, but we also saw higher mortgage rates, closer to 6 or 7 percent, rather than below 5 percent.

So if we actually *lose* money saving money and it costs us personally to save, then why save money at all? Because the personal benefits of security, stability, and reduced stress plus future financial reward (less debt, financial stability and security) outweigh the cost of keeping cash savings. It's worth the money and immediate sacrifice in the long run.

THE BENEFITS OF SAVING AND HOW TO DO IT BETTER

Saving money will save your hide. By looking at the cost of not saving, you see the benefit of saving. If you lose your job or have a drop of income in the household, you have that safety net, kind of like the ones that catch trapeze artists when they fall. Instead of painfully going kerplop, you fall, then gracefully pop right back up again to where you were. Having eight months of cash savings around can prevent you from losing your home, moving yourself and your family, losing your way of life, or even just falling behind into credit card debt that will eat away at your hard-earned dollars for years. Those savings will also be your psychological cushion. Knowing that they're there will help you relax, be healthy, focus on other things, and even say auf Wiedersehen to a job that's killing you. (This is known in some circles as FU money.)

Peace of mind is priceless. In this case, you can build your own peace of mind, and you and your family can enjoy the rewards, at a comparably small immediate cost (sacrifice, taxes, inflation).

Most of us, in response to the icy wake-up call known as the recession, have become aware of the dire need to save cash. Our savings rate as I write is around 5 percent, which is not as good as the 8 percent or so we were saving in the 1980s, but I'll take it. *So how can we save better, and more?* There are three ways.

1. Automate It

When our employers take money out of our paychecks for our benefits and retirement savings before we even see it, we tend to not miss it as much. Act like your own employer: Get the money out of your account before you even see it and before you can use it. Sign up for automated, regular withdrawals from the checking account in which you deposit your paycheck; have that money go into a savings account or money market account that pays interest. This for years now has been the best way for me to save. Particularly when you're on a very limited budget, this is one savings secret that's well suited for tight living. Just don't automate so much savings that you end up using your credit card or paying overdraft fees. No sense in that.

2. Find the Money

After you've looked at your monthly budget. I'm assuming you've done that already but if not, pull together all your receipts and bills for one month, including ATM receipts and small purchases, and tally them up into categories to see where you're spending too much and where you can cut back fairly easily; look closely at your regular monthly bills. Of course, the biggest expense for most of us is our home, which may not be a manageable expense to cut down. But if you see that your home is costing you (in mortgage payment or rent, home insurance, and property taxes and maintenance) more than around 35 percent of your take-home pay every month, you've got a big decision to make. Other pricey places to look to cut expenses and transform them into savings is the cable bill, phone bills, and utility bills. Are you paying too much for these services? Most of us are, but there's nothing like a little research and time with customer service to save another $100 a month. First, check out what the competition is offering. Then use that knowledge to call customer service for your cell phone, landline (or even consider cutting your landline altogether), Internet service, and cable bill, and ask them (nicely!) to lower your rates. After all, the competition is offering a lower amount and you really, really don't want to have to switch, but you're trying to save money in hard times! You'd be surprised how a little negotiation can put another $1,000+ a year in your pocket.

A couple other cost-cutting tools can be found online. Bookmark the following sites:

- BillShrink (www.billshrink.com)
- FatWallet (www.fatwallet.com)
- RetailMeNot (www.retailmenot.com)
- CouponMom (www.couponmom.com)
- PriceGrabber (www.pricegrabber.com)

3. Make More Money

This one is the most difficult way to boost your savings, but where there's a will and a need, this one packs a lot of juice. Bringing more money in doesn't need to be as big as working an additional twenty hours a week at unskilled labor, though if you're so inclined, go for it. Take up holiday and weekend dog walking for neighbors who need to travel, which can bring in another $100 to $200 a month that goes directly into that savings account. Depending on your skills and experience, the following freelance opportunities may bring you in some extra cash in your spare time: website design, graphic design, editing, baby-sitting, catering, and cake decorating. Or make extra money by extending your day job, such as doing your friends' taxes if you're a CPA. Just be careful. If you're not taking on an hourly weekend or evening job but instead working on your own, make sure you keep this savings work separate from your full-time job. Your full-time job comes first, then your savings job. Just make sure that the extra funds you make don't turn into extra spending; keep your life on a one-job budget and put the extra money directly into savings.

WHERE TO PUT YOUR SAVINGS

Savings need to be liquid. This means no mutual funds, no five-year CDs. Your 401(k) or IRA is not the place to put your emergency funds. The number one reason your savings exist is to protect you, so you can't invest in anything that carries risk or has restrictions on withdrawals; you want it all to be there in times of need. Emergency savings must be in an account that gives you at least dollar for dollar with twenty-four-hour access. You can dissolve an online trading account in seconds, but you can also lose a ridiculous amount of money in that account in days and have to pay capital gains taxes on your returns. For your savings to keep you stable, *they* need to be stable.

> **Two Reasons Banks Give You Money to Hold Your Money**
> - They use your money to make money.
> - To lure you into doing more business, and more profitable business, with them, like loans.

There are three main options for your liquid cash these days: a checking account, a savings account, and a money market account.

Checking Account

A checking account is too utilitarian to be effective at saving money, and most checking accounts now cost us money in monthly fees, not to mention most don't let you earn interest. But sometimes, as we build our emergency savings, little things go wrong like a plumber's visit, car repairs, and organization fees. So there is one kind of savings that you should have in a checking account: *a $500 cushion.* You don't want to have to tap your emergency savings for anything under $500, so work to keep a cushion in your checking account to buffer you from pop-up expenses.

Savings Account

We hope you can find a high-yield savings account. A savings account has the sole function of holding on to your money and growing it, slowly, by earning interest. You don't write checks off of a savings account, though you can swing money back and forth between your savings and checking if you need to, sometimes for a transfer fee. Look for a bank, credit union, or online bank that offers not only the best savings rate but easy and free transfers to your checking account and, of course, automated withdrawals from your checking account to fund it. Shop around at Bankrate (www.bankrate.com) or MoneyRates (www.money-rates.com).

Money Market Account

A money market account (MMA) sometimes offers a better rate than a plain savings account but has some of the added benefits of a checking account in that you can write checks off of your funds, if need be.

Some MMAs charge you for the privilege and/or limit how many checks you can write. Also, like some savings accounts, look out for monthly minimums. If you get charged $12 a month for having less than $2,500 in the account, that extra .05 percent in interest may not be worth it. Avoid minimum requirements as much as possible. Shop around.

Why Not CDs?

Certificates of deposit (CDs) usually offer higher interest rates than savings and money market accounts. They can do this because you agree to let the bank hold on to your money for a period of time. But this is why CDs don't qualify as liquid; hence they're probably not the best place for your emergency savings. However, if you have more than six months' worth of cash savings, you can put the rest in a six-month CD if it earns more interest than your savings account. And if you like to have up to a year or more in cash savings, you can *ladder your CDs*. This nice trick means that you put, say, $2,000 in a six-month CD this month, then another $2,000 in another six-month CD next month, and another the month after that. This means that each CD will come due month to month—the first in six months, the next in seven months, the next in eight, and so on. And if you don't need the money, you can put the money into another CD, perhaps at better rates because rates have nowhere else to go but up at this point.

The cost of not having your cash in a CD, which would earn more money than a savings account, is worth the benefit of having access to the money you need right away. If you cash out a CD before its maturity date, you can lose the interest you earned and may have to pay fees; that's too high a price to pay to gamble on a slightly better interest rate.

Real $$$ Cost of Saving Cash
Low interest rates, return
Inflation
Taxed earnings

Real Personal Cost of Saving Cash
Sacrifice
Delayed gratification
More work

Real $$$ Benefits of Saving Cash
Safety net in case of job loss, disability
Avoids debt, such as credit card debt
Maintains assets (such as home equity)

Real Personal Benefits of Saving Cash
Security, stability
Lower stress, worry, anxiety
Maintains household quality of life

The Real Cost of
Investing

Money suffocates under a mattress.

Margaret's voice was mildly shrill during her call to the show for help. She wasn't the one who just lost fifteen years' worth of retirement savings, every penny, in Lehman Brothers stock; her son had. He'd worked his way up over those years at Lehman. I had to ask Margaret why her son, someone in the finance industry, would gamble everything on one individual stock that also happened to be the company where he works. She said it was because "he believed in the company." Well, we all have convictions, but putting both your career (paycheck, income) and your retirement savings in one very, very small basket, no matter how promising the basket seems, is a hard way to find out that what you believe in can disappear.

Until 2009, it seems like we all believed that there was another Microsoft or Google out there, another company that we could bank on to grow our money into monoliths. But with the Great Recession (not to mention Enron, Worldcom, and the like), too many American investors found out the hard way that not spreading your money around can turn your potential monolith into a molehill, if that.

Margaret's son is an extreme case. But I heard from thousands of investors during the recession, including clients of Bernie Madoff and other con men and bad brokers and those who were invested in a stock market that lost over 60 percent at its low. It was an amazing time to give financial advice.

If I were to rank in order of occurrence the actions taken by folks on their retirement savings during the market crash, investors terrified by what was once an ally in building a future, those who pulled everything out of the market had to be on top. There were some very lucky folks who timed their retreat just right. But when in our lifetime have so many people pulled *all* their money out of the stock market? The stock market lost at its bottom, in March 2009, over 60 percent. But then it went back up to hit 10,000 again only eighteen months later. That's a roller-coaster ride most folks don't have the stomach for, but should we? What is the cost of investing vs. the cost of *not* investing? Where are the real costs of taking chances on a market that's not under your control?

WHY THE MATTRESS SUCKS

The biggest cost associated with investing has to do with not investing at all. Maybe you feel like you don't make enough now to put away for the future or maybe the whole idea of the market and all its potential dangers scare you. It can be an intimidating, seemingly unknowable place (there are more than twenty-four hundred individual stocks on the New York Stock Exchange alone), and it is hard to sock money away for tomorrow that you really could use today to pay bills or take a vacation. Finding the money to put away is actually the easiest hurdle to jump if that's what's preventing you from saving money for the long term. You are the gatekeeper; all you need is to open the gates. So what's keeping you?

Few of us have the gene for easily holding off on satisfaction for ten, twenty, or more years. It feels better to not have as much pressure on your budget now. To be able to instead take that money you'd save for retirement and do a little retiring on vacation this year. Or to just pay your kid's tuition and instead invest in them since you can see the results now (and they'll take care of you, right?). But the reality is that putting money away for retirement and investing it so it grows faster than a savings account *is* a form of taking care of yourself now. Every year that goes by that you don't save costs you exponentially in the future. If you don't take care of yourself, who will?

This is a conundrum where the personal and financial costs of not investing take a symbiotic toll on you. If you don't save enough money and find a safe way to both hold on to it and grow it long term, you won't have enough funds not only to retire, but to take care of you should you get too old or disabled to work. Even if you don't plan on ever retiring (I don't), you still won't be able to work at the same capacity as you always have. And then what? You end your days at the mercy of what you've saved . . . or what *little* you've saved. To spend your life thinking about what you coulda, shoulda, woulda done is much too high a price.

Good old-fashioned market pros will remind us that past performance doesn't predict the future, but so far in the history of the stock market, even after the Great Depression, a recovery always comes, and if you're not part of it, you lose. We also, as an investing nation and world, tend to fall into patterns of ten-year cycles. Why ten years? Because that's how long it takes for us to forget the foibles and lessons of the prior years. Boom and bust is the way it goes, and that can work for you as long as you invest for the long term. This roller coaster known as the stock market can cause vertigo and heart attacks, so why bother if the cost is agita and potentially large losses, even if gains match or exceed them?

Let's take the mattress vs. the market—a very simple example, assuming regular investing over twenty years. First, the biggest risks of the broad market are risks of gains and losses, sometimes swinging down 62 percent and then up 40 percent; the biggest risks of mattress stuffing include getting robbed, experiencing a fire or flood, and having uncomfortable sleeping arrangements. The only benefit of the mattress is that you can touch and feel your money, making it seem like you're keeping every penny, your principal. The mattress may win in a down stock market, but over a long period of time, the market is much more likely to win out. Let's start with $1,000; Bob puts it under his mattress, then adds $250 a month to his pile for twenty years. Inflation, acting like a hungry bedbug, chomps away at Bob's money year after year at an average rate of 3 percent. So after one year, that initial $1,000 turns into $997, and so on. And he's not earning any interest, like he would in a money market account or other interest-bearing account, so there's nothing to counter that chomp. After twenty years, all Bob has under that mattress is $45,186 of buying power. Had Bob put that money into an interest-bearing bank account (backed by the FDIC and, therefore, safe from robbers, fire, flood, and bank collapse), at an average of 1.3 percent interest, he'd have $51,329. But if Bob had put that money into the market (well-diversified investments, of course), and garnered a conservative but solid average of 7 percent in returns, he'd have $93,832 after twenty years of inflation. If you're a mattress lover, at what cost are you assuaging your fears? You're losing potentially double your money. Pricey mattress.

Margaret's son obviously paid a tremendous cost for investing his money, but it wasn't the act of investing itself that cost him, it was *what he invested in*. On top of the pyramid of possibly pricey investing mistakes, where and how you choose to invest is absolutely the potentially highest cost that you have control over. Your choice cost runs relative to risk in investing. Invest in the riskiest thing, expect the possibility of the highest cost, which is the loss of everything. Invest in the safest thing, risks and costs may be lower, but so will your returns.

As when buying a home, investing carries both a potential cost as well as benefits. You must know where the risk is and at what level as well as your appetite for risk before judging just how much you want investing to cost you. Then you can reap its benefits.

ONE BASKET

There are over five thousand individual stocks (in different exchanges) out there to choose from, but some of us choose to buy stock that's too close to home: company stock. I'll tackle this one first because it's one of the biggest investing losers I've encountered, at much too high a personal cost and all too easy to avoid.

Losing everything to Lehman Brothers or Enron tanking are extremes. But I continue to be surprised by how many people regularly

> To really understand risk, you must wrap your head around **probability**: what can or cannot happen—in all permutations—plus what influences what could happen and why.
>
> This is not accounting but statistics.

put essential retirement money into the entity that also pays them. Investing in the company you work for by buying and holding its individual stock is one of the riskiest stock moves of all because it has little to do with accounting and a lot to do with *probability*, or odds. The choices you have in your retirement benefits are supposed to be diverse to decrease the odds that you'll get taken for all of it which is why you don't see any other individual stocks in your choices. But so far, no new rules have come about to change the fact that company stock is allowed to be the only individual stock offered in employee-benefit retirement plans: Buy some and bolster up the company! You believe in us! Dangerous stuff.

You already get your income, your paycheck, and a block of your career from the company you work for. Putting your retirement money in the company stock is *dangerous on two levels*:

- You're not diversifying where your money comes from (you get money from the company and you're putting money back into the company expecting it to pay you twice, or more).
- We cannot possibly know all the machinations going on at a company that we do not own, and we have little say in how it's run, even if at executive levels, which is why investing in any individual stock is tremendously risky.

But surely I don't work for an Enron or Lehman! Neither did I, or my friends, when we became victims of the Time Warner-AOL merger-gone-wrong. One of my dear friends was a potential retiree. As layoffs started up, she was offered a buyout package with the stock at around $60 a share. Thank high heaven she took it. She had the majority of her retirement savings in the stock, and that price per share enabled her to retire comfortably. On the flip side, those who decided not to take the buyout (and the remainder of us who had been awarded vested stock options over time) soon saw their money dwindle to as little as $12 a share. So let's say you had thirty thousand vested stock options that you decided to take at $60 a share. That's $1.8 million. At $12 a share? That's $360,000. Which could you retire on?

Of course, what if you worked at Microsoft when it had its IPO in 1986, with shares opening at $21 and you held on through nine stock splits (several times the stock went over $100 or even $150)? Well, maybe you'd be one of the twelve thousand millionaires the company has created as employees and investors, but most likely not. To replicate something like that, the following events would have to happen:

- You hold the stock long enough to ride out the bumps in value (meaning, the price goes up, waaaay up from the original price of your purchase).
- You don't sell your stock or cash out your options at the wrong time.
- As an employee you are awarded stock options and/or have access to stock (in your 401(k)) and your vested awards become fully vested at a good time for the stock price.
- You work at a company with the mega-returns and promise of Microsoft.

Your odds stink. It's too much a matter of *timing* when you buy or sell, plus the *company's performance*, plus your *ability to keep your job* at said company. If you're willing and able to swallow the potential costs of risking it all, just know that you have a much higher chance of becoming like Margaret's son (broke and starting over at thirty-six) than you have of becoming one of Microsoft's millionaires.

I own company stock. But hundreds of different company stocks. That's what mutual and index funds and exchange traded funds (ETFs) do for you. You probably also know that bonds are sometimes less risky than stocks (depends on what type of bond and grade) and that Treasury instruments like TIPS and T-bills are backed dollar for dollar by the U.S. government, so you've got nothing to lose but earnings (very low now, 1 to 2 percent). But after steering clear of wrapping yourself up in a blanket of company stock or individual stocks alone, the riskiest and costliest moves we make when investing are actually about *timing* when and how we buy and sell as well as *what* we buy and sell.

TIMING

So how about all those folks who pulled out of the stock market before it hit bottom? They were the winners, right? Not exactly. You not only have to time your way out of a tanking market but also have to time your way back in. After all, even after the Great Depression, the best periods of growth in the stock market have been within the five years after a stock market low/recession. The cost of not timing your exit and entrance into the market or particular investment can mean thousands of dollars over time. For example, what if someone pulled their funds out of the market just after its height, just as the Dow was headed down to 13,000 in January 2008? Had she kept her funds in cash, she would have avoided the additional losses the market took as it went down to 7,000 in February 2009. But has this person gotten back in again? As I write, the Dow is around 10,000, so there have been hefty gains, but we're far from another 13,000. But the real cost of sitting this ride out is that once the market goes back up, she'll have lost out on gains.

> **Disposition Effect**
>
> We tend to sell winners too early and losers too late. We're human.

And what about if, instead of Mr. 13K, we look at the thousands of people who pulled billions out of the stock market by the bottom of the crash. Let's say some got tired of losing when the Dow was at 8,000 and then got too scared to get back in. The cost of this timing is around 40 percent of their original investment and climbing as the market digs its way out.

That's the cost (and danger) of timing. Some of us are smart enough—or lucky enough—to time selling investments right, but the majority of us have trouble with both timing our way out and timing our way back in. The best way to increase your odds is to do two things: Invest long term (for ten years or more) and average the cost of your way in and out.

Why ten years or more? Because the longer you stay in the market (nearly any market, including housing), the more you increase your odds of making, and keeping, a return. For example, not including the most recent stock market fall, since the 1970s we've experienced six bear (negative) market periods but we've then followed each with six bull (positive) markets, and growth has outstripped the losses. But the bear markets ran from 87 days (1990) to 929 days (2000 to 2002), and then their recovery periods, the bull markets, ran from 3,452 days (1990 to 2000) to 710 days (1974 to 1976). So to make sure that you don't end up on the bear end of the market, staying put helps. Even if you factor in the enormous losses we sustained in the Great Recession, if you had been in the market for ten years before the low in February 2009 (when the Dow was at 7,092), staying put another twelve months when the Dow came back over 10,000 would have allowed you to make better than mattress money since you got in closer to 9,000 in 1999. Ten years means you make money, sometimes only some money but usually much money.

Another important part of staying in the market is not trying to sell and buy when the market starts going up and down. We miss some of the best trading days by trying to time our investments and risk much too high a cost; those who pulled out at the biggest fall are an extreme example. The management firm Legg Mason offers a great analysis of what happens when you miss the best days of the market, and you'd be surprised: As little as ten days out of twenty years can cost you tens of thousands of dollars or more. For example, if you had invested $10,000 on New Year's Eve of 1988 and kept it in the market through twenty years, on the same day in 2008, you'd end up with almost $54,000. If you had missed only the top ten days of trading in that twenty-year period, you'd have almost $30,000 *less*. If you missed the top thirty days, you'd have only $11,252 (those twenty days cost you around $43,000!). We don't know what the best days in the market are until they happen. You can make adjustments to your portfolio, such as putting another 10 percent in cash or more stable government bonds, especially if your stomach (and heart) can't handle the market volatility, but just don't get completely out of the market. A long-term strategy may not be sexy, but it helps you earn more and that costs less than sexy.

Also not high on the sexy list, but super-high on the list of tried-and-true make-money tools, is a wonky thing called dollar cost averaging (DCA). Accounting-speak may put you to sleep, but the concept behind DCA, as I'll now call it, is eye-opening.

Imagine you have to buy a box of cereal. Now imagine that the price of that box of cereal changes every day, several times a day, and not by a little, but by a lot. Last month it cost $4.35 at close of day, but today it costs $2.78 at noon. You have to buy your growing family twenty boxes of cereal at the lowest possible total cost over the next six months. But the cereal has been as low as $1.35 a box and as high as $7.80 a box, so how do you know that if you buy five boxes today, at $2.78, that you'll get the right price? Well, past performance rarely predicts future performance with accuracy; just because the price of that box went up last month doesn't mean that it'll go up again next month. Since you don't need all the cereal all at once, you choose to buy five boxes today at $2.78 and buy another bunch of boxes next month at, you hope, a lower price.

Now imagine keeping track of a thousand or more boxes of cereal, each fluctuating at different prices. And you want to buy each of them at the best, lowest cost. How can you possibly keep track of thousands of cereal prices and buy them each at the right time? You can't, really. Who the heck has time to do that? So what you can do to increase the odds that you'll beat CouponMom (www.couponmom.com) at this game is to buy a portion of what you need at different times over a certain period. That's DCA, or dollar cost averaging.

Go Against the Grain with Your Gut

When my husband and I started our simplified employee pension (SEP) accounts, the tax-friendly way to save for the self-employed and business owners, the market was at 13,000 and climbing. Everyone was yelling, "Buy! Buy!" but my gut was saying "Hell, no." I had experienced enough bubbles in my lifetime to smell a burst coming. I kept our SEPs in cash through the crash and avoided a nearly 50 percent loss. However, I could have been wrong—after all, I missed out on another over 1,000 market gain, so my gut did cost us something. It's the only time in my life that I've market timed. I was faced with a scenario that few of us have ever seen in our lifetimes—a serious money-gouging bubble for buyers.

Your gut will not tell you to jump onto the hottest investment opportunity that you saw on late-night TV or one that your dad's broker whispers to you. That's all in your head. Your gut reacts to threats, and that sometimes makes it worth listening to.

The stock market moves up, down, and sideways on a daily basis. If you bought all your holdings on one day, you'd lock in that day's prices, and they may not be the best. And if you took all your money out in one day, you'd lock in that day's prices as well, which truly may not be the best. DCA also works better than trying to time the market because we as human beings kind of stink at judging when to buy and sell. Individual investors especially have a proven tendency to let losing investments fester for too long (But what if it goes up? we think) and we don't let winners win long enough (I'm going to cut my losses). So DCA does two things for us when we need to either buy or sell investments: It *smoothes out* the market's tendency to fluctuate widely in small periods of time, and our tendency to misjudge when to move in and out.

The number one place we all tend to DCA is in our employee-sponsored retirement plans, such as 401(k)s and 403(b)s. And that's a good thing. If you have chosen to put a portion of every paycheck into your retirement plan, which you have distributed throughout investment options, you are practicing DCA. Every paycheck buys a portion of the market at a different level and different period of time. So those of you who kept your savings in the market *and* kept contributing to your retirement during the market bust bought the market on sale! And that's the good news for those who started their 401(k)s or other retirement savings during the recent market low. Everything was on sale, and you're the most likely to have no place to go but up. Of course, you may say that that offers no solace to those close to retirement who had to take such a big hit with little time to recover. This is true, but you should be scheduling yourself nearly out of the market as you near retirement, especially if you're in retirement.

Reality Check

If you look at investing numbers at the bottom of the market drop in 2009, a portfolio of stocks would have performed much worse than a portfolio of bonds over the same time period, let's say ten years.

But after market busts comes subsequent growth, so if you stay in the stock market even just a bit, over the long term you're most likely to outpace the bond market.

> Bonds are a wonderful hedge against a wildly pitching stock market, but for us regular folks, we need a mix of both to grow our money over time.

How can you lower the cost of getting hit by a big market drop when you need your money most, in or close to retirement? By hedging your bets (also known as *diversifying*) and *fixing* your mix on a regular basis. No one should have 100 percent of their long-term savings in the stock market. The stock market, even blue-chip stocks that seem to barely budge, is an aggressive form of investing. We need it to make our money grow faster than inflation, but like a sword (or debt), we must wield it as a potentially dangerous tool.

Consider the stock market your frenemy. We all have frenemies, and we tend to have them because we need them. The market can be your friend and grow your money like nothing else, but it can also leave you high and dry; hence you need to know just how much risk you're taking with this friendship. If you choose to not put any of your money in the market, you stand to lose potentially large gains, possibly 15 percent or more over the long term. If the market scares you that much and you feel better not playing this game, just realize the missed opportunity of going with your gut. It can be a costly move to avoid the market, but one that's worthwhile to you.

I won't get too wonky with charts, graphs, and accounting on diversification since bigger costs are to come, but there are a few questions that can help you make the right decisions when you see a list of available investing options for your 401(k) or other investment account:

- How much time do you have? (Must be more than ten years.)
- How's your stomach for this stuff? (If you get sick every time the market has a bad day, then you shouldn't play with this frenemy more than you can bear.)
- How much money are you expecting to make? (Determine your expected returns.)

So, what's diversification and why and how does it save you money? Diversification means spreading your investments around (known as *asset allocation*) in such a way as to reconcile the three tenants I listed earlier: your stomach for risk, your time frame, and the returns you'd like to see. No, investing in ten different stocks is not diversification. No, investing in ten different bonds is not diversification. You need diversity of levels of *risk*, not *things*. For instance, you know company stock is very, very risky, and you'd like to not see your money totally disappear, so don't put more than 5 percent of your money in individual stocks; bet only what you can afford to lose.

To lower the cost of risk in your stock investments, one of the best innovations out there is *index funds*. These beauts will come up again in this chapter because they offer some of the lowest cost diversification around. Index funds follow a fixed list of stocks so you can find ones as basic as the S&P 500 or as specialized as a tech sector index. Because they follow in-

> **Know and Understand What You're Investing In**
>
> This advice alone can and will save you a tremendous amount of potential costs and can greatly improve not only the performance of your investments over time but your ability to manage them and sleep at night, which is well worth the cost of sitting down once in a while with an investing guide (I recommend *The Little Book of Common Sense Investing* by Jack Bogle; yes, I'm a Boglehead) to get a basic grip on the risk factors of where your money is vs. where it should be.

dexes and are not actively fiddled around with by a fund manager, as with regular mutual funds (managers buy and sell within the fund on a regular basis), you save a chunk in management fees. However, index funds run different rates of risk and diversification as well. A general index fund like the S&P 500 is a pool of five hundred stocks of various companies scattered across sectors and industries. But an index fund that follows only gold industry stocks or tech stocks is only as diverse as the sector, so you have to diversify still further.

The cost of not spreading your risk around is seen in Margaret's son, who put all his eggs in one basket. Diversification—where your mix should help you reach your goals—begs the question: Just how risky do you want to be? Let's settle on some *rules of diversification* that will lower the cost of investing over time:

- The younger you are and the further away you are from retirement, the more you can afford to risk; time is on your side to ride out stock market swings. But still, putting 80 percent or more of your money in the stock market is super-risky and not for the faint of heart (or for me).
- When you're more than twenty years away from retirement, your job is to grow your money so you need to take on more risk; less risk will cost you over the long term.
- When you get closer to retirement, your job is to protect more of your money; you need to lower your exposure to risk. When you're heading toward ten to fifteen years before you retire, start shifting down your stock market exposure to wind down your risk and cost. Use DCA to move out over the rest of your life: 2 percent into bonds or cash this year, another 2 percent the next, and so on.

- You don't need *all* your money at age sixty-five or when you retire; don't panic if you're set to retire and the market is not on your side. *Panic costs money!* It may be a matter of adjusting your goals and holding off a year or two before getting out of the market to increase your odds of recouping your losses. Remember, five years out of every recession there are substantial gains.

- Knowledge lowers costs. Find out what your mutual funds in your retirement holdings are actually invested in. Which stocks? Are there too many overlapping sectors or repeat stocks in your portfolio? Those repeats and overlaps cost in lower diversification. If I ask you what are you invested in, would you know? Once you know, you can make moves that will save you money.

- You should always have some cash in your retirement portfolio, say 5 to 10 percent or more as you get closer to retirement. Cash holdings help buoy up the losing parts of your portfolio—for example, when stocks are down (cash meant my losses from the big 2009 drop were about 4 percent less than they could have been—that's 4 percent savings).

Diversification in Action (Balancing Risk)

This chart is tremendously oversimplified but useful for showing how when one part of your portfolio is performing badly, other parts of your portfolio will lessen your losses... if you are diversified.

When the markets go down:			When the markets go up:		
⬇	⬇	⬆	⬆	⬆	⬇
Bonds	Stock	Cash	Bonds	Stock	Cash

One of the biggest costs of investing is misjudging risk. Diversification helps counter too much risk; not trying to time the market helps keep more of your money and fees down; understanding what you own and where your money is helps you make better investing decisions that cost you less in lost revenue or, in the case of a company or money manager gone bad, keeps you from losing it all.

There are two more investing costs that have little to do with what you think is a hot sector and a lot to do with how you manage where your money is and with whom: taxes and fees.

TAXES

In the last chapter, I reviewed how it costs money to save money, one of those costs being the taxes you pay on the interest you make every year. The same concept applies to investing. This is a cost that most of us can avoid, as long as we're saving for the long term, such as for retirement. No, I'm not talking about tax dodging!

When someone asks me, via phone, email, or Facebook, where he should put his money, my first question is to determine what that person is saving for (a long-term or short-term goal) and if he has access to tax-friendly retirement accounts. Any investing goal under five years shouldn't touch the stock market, unless you're just a crazy cowboy (and ready to lose). But if you're looking at investing for long-term goals, such as retirement or your kid's college, you have to know that using an IRA is the only way to truly maximize your investing.

Let's start with a basic, no-frills investment that you make on your own, outside of an IRA, so it's taxed (let's say at a withdrawal rate of

15 percent). Let's say you also have a 401(k), which isn't taxed as it grows, but is taxed when you withdraw it (meaning it is tax deferred), and a Roth IRA, which is taxed before it grows but never sees taxes again (it is tax-free). If you start with $20,000 and add $250 a month, at a conservative 7 percent return over twenty years, the taxable investment (your individual mutual fund, for example) will give you $170,000 after taxes, whereas your 401(k) turns into $186,000 tax deferred and your Roth IRA is a mighty $219,000, which is tax-free! **An almost $50,000 difference in outcome all because of taxes.** That's a pretty hard track record to beat, if you think that you can do better on your own than what your 401(k) has to offer you or if you're just not interested in a Roth IRA. Much too high a cost. There are other things to consider with tax-friendly retirement tools, such as income limits and withdrawal restrictions, but in regard to taxes, each has benefits and costs to consider. Keep them in mind and see which (probably several) work best for you (for more information see the IRS website at www.irs.gov).

- **401(k), 403(b), 457.** Contributions are tax deductible; pretax money; taxes paid in retirement, when taken as income.
- **Traditional IRA.** Contributions are tax deductible (income restrictions); post-tax money; taxes paid in retirement, when taken as income.
- **Roth IRA.** Contributions are not tax deductible; post-tax money; no taxes paid in retirement.
- **SEP, Keogh, SIMPLEs.** Contributions are tax deductible; pretax money; taxes paid in retirement, when taken as income.

FEES

I was waiting to do a regular live hit on the local news when a young producer named Tom saddled up to me and asked if I minded answering a couple of quick questions. Tom's wife was expecting a baby, and they wanted to work on college savings as well as estate planning. He had been working with a financial adviser, whom he inherited from his parents, but this adviser didn't really understand tax-friendly college savings vehicles, like 529s. I was happy to help, but as soon as he mentioned inheriting the adviser from his parents, I had to ask, "Do you know how he gets paid?" Interestingly enough, Tom was a very well-versed personal finance guy. But his eyebrows went up as he realized, "Man, I don't know!" I explained to Tom that the reason I asked is because first of all he seemed unhappy that this adviser didn't know how to guide him, especially regarding tax advantages, but that outside of taxes, another costly killer of returns are fees.

Let's say you're currently racking up a total of 1.75 percent in fees in your 401(k). But your Roth IRA is in an index fund, and your service fee is only 0.5 percent. You have $30,000 in each, and you add $300 a month to each for the next fifteen years for an average return of 7 percent. Those 401(k) fees will leave you with a bit over $150,000 after fifteen years, whereas your low-fee Roth IRA with 1.25 percent fewer fees will get you more than another $10,000 in returns, putting you over $160,000. Seems small, but that's only over fifteen years; most of us invest for much longer than that, and the longer we invest, the more those fees cost us.

There are great free fee calculators at Dinky town.net (www.dinkytown.net). Click on "Investing Calculators."

Financial institutions and products are a fee fest, and until recently, many of us didn't realize just how much we were paying in fees in our retirement savings and investments. There are multiple layers of fees, so read through the following sections and do a little fee finding of your own. How much are you paying in fees on your investments right now? Which fees are worthwhile to you? (Say, your financial planner.) And which fees can you get rid of to lower your costs?

Mutual Fund Management Fees

Regular mutual funds can have some great returns but they are actively managed, which means a team or person trades in and out of your fund to try to maximize returns. You get saddled with the cost of management, anywhere from 0.5 percent to 2 percent. Mutual funds can also charge sales fees and commissions as *front-end* or *back-end loads* (meaning the fee is taken out when you initially buy into the fund or when you sell) as well as *Rule 12b-1 fees*. Think of 12b-1s as the way some fund companies pay for business costs, such as advertising or marketing.

401(k) Fees

There are three kinds of 401(k) fees: *plan administration fees* (which find their way to you either through a flat fee or a portion of what you invest), *investment fees* (which are fund management fees), and *individual service fees* (which tend to come into play if, for example, you borrow from your 401(k)).

Loads, Commissions, Sales Fees

Loads, commissions, and sales fees are tied to a percentage of what you buy or sell.

So how can you avoid these fees? Most 401(k) providers now must reveal up front how much you're paying in fees for the benefit. You may be able to move your money into a lower-fee fund that replicates the investments you're happy with, but be careful of breaking up with one fund with fees to one with lower fees if you're not happy with what's inside that fund. *You must balance fees with function*, what's inside the investment and how it relates to what's in your portfolio.

Look for keywords (most searches you can do online) in regard to your investments: *load* and *12b-1* and *fees*. Some fees are avoidable but some, like your 401(k) plan administration fee, may not be. You can also compare the loads as well as the performance and content of many mutual funds at sites like Morningstar (www.morn ingstar.com). But one of the best ways to avoid the cost of management fees, service fees, and commissions is to invest in an *index fund*. Index funds follow just indexes; they don't need management or service, and many are available that replicate what good fund managers do.

Is it worth paying someone else to manage your investments? That depends on who it is and how he or she gets paid. **Brokers paid with commission** tend to be the most expensive. They are not required to act in your sole interest (as fiduciaries). This means a commission-based broker or planner may push products and investments on you that make him, not necessarily you, money. Also, he doesn't deal with your other assets, such as your home, other real estate, and insurance policies.

So what about **fee-based financial planners**? They are required to act as fiduciaries—in your best interest. But are they worth what you pay them in terms of better returns? Depends on their skills, their policies, their record, and how much *you* know and communicate. Increase your odds of getting your money's worth by screening well who you hire (start at the Security and Exchange Commission's website, www.sec.gov), check out fees, and get referrals—try the Financial Planning Association (www.fpanet.org) or the National Association of Personal Financial Advisors (www.napfa.org). Don't look necessarily for Madoff-like predictable returns so much as her approach toward your money and investing in general. And watch out for yes-men; too many planners will just do what you want them to do because they want your business, rather than challenge you when you're doing something wrong. Keep your sniffer open to too much yes. Sometimes the best advisers will challenge you to get you the best return.

Let's forget about all that math and all those rules for a bit and turn the focus onto ourselves and why we do what we do. Hundreds of personal finance experts and writers and planners can tell you what you *need* to do, but what do you really end up doing and why?

INERTIA

Remember that SEP I mentioned that I kept all in cash just before the stock market collapse? Well, when the market went below 8,000, I should have (and I knew this) started putting that money into the market in a well-diversified portfolio. But did I? I did not; in fact, it wasn't until the market was much higher that I got back in. Why? No time. Not an immediate pressing priority. Not on the top of my to-do list.

But why didn't I make it top of my to-do list when I know how important it is to our finances and future chances of retiring at the level we want to be? Because it's too easy to put off what seems like a faraway goal. We get bogged down with immediate costs and needs. This is why many of us fall prey to the cost of what I'll call *inertia*. You'd think that doing what I do for a living means that every facet of my financial life is run to a T. But personally, I'd rather help others with their life, their questions, their money, and their portfolio than deal with my own.

Our personalities are a driving force in how we invest, so knowing yourself and facing your feelings about investing reduces the cost of not investing at all or the right way. You could add up all the costs of taking on too much risk or too little risk, plus taxes plus fees, and you may not even come close to the cost of not investing because you just don't wanna or because you feel like you just can't.

I'll take care of it later. That's inertia summed up—procrastination, but without a real and true deadline. With investing, especially when you have access to employer-based retirement accounts and everything's on autopilot, it can be incredibly easy to not pay any attention once those forms are filled out. And some of us don't want to pay attention (though I surmise that you'd be very unlikely to be reading this book if that were the case). *But not paying attention costs money.* That cost, however, is too easily put off because our goal seems so far away—retirement. Instead, think of your investing goals in yearly increments, and develop a plan for how you're going to increase contributions, fix your mix over time, roll that darn old 401(k) over, and so forth. For most of us, bringing a long-term goal like retirement into an immediate or soon-to-be reality or goal can help break the binds of inertia.

Remember how much those ten days lost in a twenty-year market cost? It's a tremendous amount of money, especially in comparison to what you initially invest. Think about what's keeping you from looking into your retirement money or what's keeping you from putting any away at all. The only thing that should be keeping you from contributing to your retirement is unemployment or drastic lack of income. In that case, your immediate needs greatly outstrip the cost of lost opportunity.

If numbers help, let's look at how much inertia can cost you:

- What if you invested $250 every month from age twenty-five to age sixty-five at an average 8 percent return? You'll have a balance near $884,638 at the end.
- What if you wait until you're thirty to start saving or putting your money into investments with stronger returns than a

money market ($250 a month at 8 percent to age sixty-five)? You'll have $581,366 at the end.

Those five years cost you over $300,000, or over $60,000 a year, and more than $5,000 a month! Few of us are rich enough to miss $5,000 a month. Seeing how much inertia costs you in real terms should help you into motion. That $300,000 three decades from now is a cost way too far away to feel. But five Gs a month right now, that should hurt. And remember, it's not the ages I used for the comparison that matter as much as your time frame. When it comes to compound interest, which is one of the most amazing ways to make money, time is truly on your side. Those first five years you save, for example, you'll only have $18,864 to show for it, so how does five years at the end cost you $300,000? Because compound interest goes into sixth gear as it approaches the horizon and as more money piles up and grows exponentially (think $2 \times 2 = 4$, $4 \times 4 = 16$, $16 \times 16 = 256 \ldots$). Compound interest is money earned on money earned—for example: You have $1,000 and in one month earn $1.35 on it so now your balance is $1,001.35. The next month you earn interest on this higher balance (granted, not that much higher yet). The next month, it's an even bigger balance that your interest earnings are applied to. And so on and so on. This is why inertia can hurt you so much with investing; the power lies more with time frame than the amount of money you put in. The longer you can build and grow, the more you'll have.

LACK OF CONFIDENCE

"I don't know what I'm doing so I'll just put 10 percent into everything going down the list." I've heard this scenario way too often. And more often than not, it has to do with a mind-set that says, "Not my thing." It may not be your thang, but it is your money. Don't let your lack of confidence leave you with less in your pocket during retirement. Read and research, just as you're doing now, to bolster up your confidence. What are your investment options? How nervous are you about the market? With so much easy access to information, there is little reason to not give yourself a primer on where your money is and where, maybe, it *should* be. What's in that global fund? What's my fee structure? Your job is not to know how to manage everyone else's portfolio but to deal with your own: your needs, your means, your future, and your gut. Only knowledge and plain ol' common sense can and should give you confidence in investing. Everyone can understand the basics, and if not, do like my friends do to me: Get someone to explain it to you for free—a friend who has a knack for it, a family member—but it's not advice you're looking for as much as knowledge of terms, opportunities, and risks. Take your knowledge from several sources, sort through what you find, and match it up with your goals and your gut. Then adjust your portfolio accordingly. And don't let anyone tell you that you can't do it. The cost is too high.

OVERCONFIDENCE

And then there are you guys who think you can beat the market. Why not? You're smart and talk to the right people and subscribe to the newsletters and all that. You must know better than us folks who preach things like long-term investing. No way, José. Study after study shows that overconfidence in investing leads to losing money. This is because overconfidence gets in the way of a buy and hold strategy, and more trades means more lost returns. Not only is this about missing out on some very valuable trading days and getting in and out at the right time; it's about at one extreme putting all your money into one stock you believe in, like Margaret's son, and at the other extreme not getting any help or looking into what your investment options really are because you think you know already. I cannot tell you how many times I've encountered men (and yes, men are much more likely to be overconfident and trade too much than women) who've asked me, so what's the next hottest stock? I don't care. Is it a hot stock because it's in a growing market sector? Do I have exposure to that sector in my portfolio? That's what you want to know and that's what I make sure to know, because in the long term, that's what matters.

Trading in and out of individual stocks, commodities, and funds can be lots of fun, like Vegas. But it's fun that costs. If you have fun money, go for it. You may hit the jackpot, but the odds are with the house. Long-term studies comparing portfolios have shown that the losses incurred from overactive trading can lead to spreads of 3 percent to 20 percent compared to portfolios that stick to a specific buy and hold strategy over time. I may not be able to convince the most macho on this one, but as long as you leave this paragraph understanding that overconfident overtrading turns the markets into a casino, rather than a long-term strategy, I'm satisfied.

Why so overconfident? We're human. We want shortcuts. We think we see patterns where there may not be any, thus leading us to think we've got a handle on the next big thing. We also tend to follow market action, getting pulled toward investments that may already be overvalued, such as gold, rather than sleuthing out the sleepers that have yet to hit the gas and, therefore, are filled with much more earning potential. And some of us love the drama of seeing numbers go up and down, all we hope with the potential to make us rich. Actually, the majority of us are risk averse, which is why we're more likely to be underconfident than overconfident. In reality, however, both approaches cost money.

BRINGING IN THE PROS?

I was lucky enough to have several Bernie Madoff victims on the show. More than anything, of course, I wanted to help them, but a question I had for each (which was more about helping the rest of us) was, "Did you know where your money was invested?" They all said no or that he'd send them statements and they'd see company names like Microsoft. But they also all said that he was getting these spectacular returns year after year, so they trusted him with where their money was going. Though Madoff did produce supposed statements, had his clients checked up themselves on what the statements said, they would have found that no, they actually didn't own those shares of Microsoft, or whichever company. There is always a danger in handing over your money to someone else to invest. The big danger is that they'll invest it badly, but that can't happen if you're paying attention. To avoid taking a blind eye to what your broker, adviser, planner, or brother-in-law is doing, you need to always know and ask: "Where is my money?"

Investing with a pro shouldn't be a one-way street where you just supply the money and he or she puts it somewhere. It needs to be a discussion and collaboration. It boils down to taking the responsibility for your money. An investing pro should be used to *help you* make decisions, not necessarily to make the decisions for you. Request not only monthly statements but schedule phone calls and meetings to discuss strategy. And definitely keep Tom in mind: How is this person getting paid? You can have a fantastic and trustworthy investing pro working for you, but if he or she is getting paid too much or the wrong way, no level of performance is going to take care of losing 3 percent or more in interest on your money every year. You can't afford to *not* invest. But for investing to not cost you too much you have to overcome inertia, educate yourself into some confidence about what you're doing, check out anyone and everyone who manages your money, diversify right, and take advantage of tax-friendly tools. Most of all, you must feel comfortable about where you put your money so it can both grow and protect you and your future.

Real $$$ Cost of Investing	Real Personal Cost of Investing
Fewer funds for discretionary spending	Distress over investment choices
Possible losses due to investment choices	Distress over market losses
Investing fees (fund management fees, administration fees)	

Real $$$ Benefits of Investing	Real Personal Benefits of Investing
Possibility to build sufficient income for retirement, remainder of life	Secure retirement, future goals
Ability to grow funds over the long term, enough to outgrow inflation, tax rates	Build wealth to enjoy in life or transfer to other family, make donations

ADDITIONAL READING
AND RESOURCES

The Real Cost of Home

Ian Ayres, "Recourse, Of Course," Freakonomics, *New York Times*, November 25, 2008, http://freakonomics.blogs.nytimes.com/tag/martin-feldstein. Interesting debate on the financial repercussions of walking away from a mortgage, aka foreclosing on purpose.

Dinkytown.net. Look for "Refinance Calculator" to see how much you'd save (or not) on refinancing. Note that dragging out the loan (say, going from twenty years left to thirty) may save you money each month but maybe not over the life of the loan (total interest paid).

Freddie Mac, "30-Year Fixed-Rate Mortgages Since 1971," www.freddiemac.com/pmms/pmms30.htm. See how mortgage rates have changed since 1971—the 1980s were brutal.

MakingHomeAffordable.gov. The government site to get help if you're struggling paying your mortgage, via the U.S. Department of Housing and Urban Development (HUD).

Bill Marsh, "The History of Home Values," *New York Times*, August 26, 2006, http://graphics8.nytimes.com/images/2006/08/26/weekinreview/27leon_graph2.large.gif. A fantastic graph, compiled by Robert Schiller (of Case-Schiller Home Price Index fame), that shows just how dramatically (and then sometimes snoozingly) home prices have fluctuated since the 1890s. Sobering.

StandardandPoors.com. Click on "S&P/Case-Schiller Home Price Indices" then click on "Fact Sheet" (pdf) for a comparison of how the housing market did from 2000 to 2009 compared to stocks and bonds. Remember, the past does not predict the future and that's only nine years as opposed to ten. In 2010, stocks boomed while home values continued to fall in many areas.

U.S. Census Bureau, "Median and Average Square Feet of Floor Area in New Single-Family Houses Completed by Location," http://www.census.gov/const/C25Ann/sftotalmedavgsqft.pdf. My, how we've grown! Into living in, buying, and building giant homes, that is. Historic record of the average square footage of an American home from 1973 to 2009.

U.S. Department of Housing and Urban Development, "Let FHA Loans Help You," www.hud.gov/buying/loans.cfm. More information on Federal Housing Authority (FHA) loans—low-down-payment loans backed by the government.

Zillow.com and Trulia.com. If you're looking for a way to compare home values either on your block or across the country, both sites offer user-friendly options to search.

The Real Cost of Marriage and Divorce

Nolo.com and LegalZoom.com. For basic, free information on divorce, the laws, your rights, and mediation.

Pew Research Center, "Millennials: A Portrait of Generation Next," February 24, 2010, http://pewresearch.org/millennials. Report with results on marriage polling.

Pew Research Center, "Women, Men and the New Economics of Marriage," January 19, 2010, http://pewsocialtrends.org/pubs/750/new-economics-of-marriage. Another fascinating Pew Research report.

TheKnot.com. Wedding, engagement, and honeymoon site with resources and ideas for spending less.

University of Michigan, "The Early Years of Marriage Project: Publications," http://projects.isr.umich.edu/eym/publications.html. Published pieces on everything from race, family ties, predicting divorce, and "newlywed narratives."

University of Virginia, "The National Marriage Project," www.virginia.edu/marriageproject. Includes study results on cohabitation, divorce, the recession's effect on marriage rates and divorce, and so forth. Note: Take results with a grain of salt.

U.S. Internal Revenue Service, "Publication 504: Divorced or Separated Individuals," 2009, www.irs.gov/publications/p504/index.html. The page to go to regarding tax rules and rights for divorced and/or separated individuals.

Elizabeth Warren, "The Middle Class on the Precipice: Rising Financial Risks for American Families," *Harvard Magazine* (January–February 2006), http://harvardmagazine.com/2006/01/the-middle-class-on-the-html. From Harvard professor Elizabeth Warren and her Consumer Bankruptcy Project.

Elizabeth Warren and Amelia Warren Tyagi, *The Two-Income Trap: Why Middle-Class Mothers and Fathers Are Going Broke* (New York: Basic Books, 2003). An unbelievably powerful book that paints a stark picture as to what's ahead for the American family if current economic trends and policy continue.

The Real Cost of Family

BabyCenter.com, "Cost of Raising a Child Calculator," www.babycenter.com/cost-of-raising-child-calculator.

BabyCenter.com, "First-Year Baby Costs Calculator," www.babycenter.com/babyCostCalculator.htm.

Bruce Bradbury, "Time and the Cost of Children," University of Michigan, National Poverty Center Working Paper Series, April 2005, www.npc.umich.edu/publications/workingpaper05/paper04/BradburyTimeCosts_NPC.pdf.

B. D. Doss et al., "The Effect of the Transition to Parenthood on Relationship Quality: An 8-Year Prospective Study," *Journal of Personality and Social Psychology* 96, no. 3 (March 2009): 601–19. The report that revved up the brouhaha that having children greatly lowers marital happiness.

Google Scholar, http://scholar.google.com/scholar?q=motherhood+wage+penalty&hl=en&as_sdt=0&as_vis=1&oi=scholart. List of and links to academic papers (pdf) on the "motherhood wage penalty."

Sharon Jayson, "Delaying Kids May Prevent Financial 'Motherhood Penalty,'" *USA Today*, April 16, 2010, www.usatoday.com/money/perfi/2010-04-15-Having-kids-early-economic-penalty15_ST_N.htm. Recent findings that the motherhood wage penalty declines and even disappears with age.

National Alliance for Caregiving, www.caregiving.org. Resources and information on caring for elderly parents.

NORC Blueprint, www.norcblueprint.org. Information on naturally occurring retirement communities and how an aging parent may qualify for local community assistance.

Garey Ramey and Valerie A. Ramey, "The Rug Rat Race," National Bureau of

Economic Research, August 2009, www.nber.org/papers/w15284. How much time we spend on childcare and why.

University of Southern California, "For Parents, Love and Money Never End," Longitudinal Study of Generations, www.usc.edu/dept/gero/research/4gen/beth.htm. On the "gratitude dividend" that kids pay parents who help them financially.

U.S. Department of Labor, "The Family and Medical Leave Act (FMLA)," www.dol.gov/compliance/laws/comp-fmla.htm. Your rights regarding taking time off to care for an aging parent or other family member.

Anne E. Winkler and Thomas R. Ireland, "Time Spent in Household Management: Evidence and Implications," University of Missouri-St. Louis, December 5, 2007, www.umsl.edu/~winklera/FOR%20web%20page%2012-05-07%20JFEI%20.pdf. The report that attempts to quantify just how much time we spend managing our households.

The Real Cost of College

The College Board, "College Cost Calculator," http://apps.collegeboard.com/fincalc/college_cost.jsp.

FinAid.org. Loaded resource for information and guidance on student loans, grants, and scholarships.

House Education and Labor Committee, "College Cost Reduction and Access Act," http://edlabor.house.gov/publications/20070905ConfReportOnePager.pdf.

Ron Lieber, "Placing the Blame as Students Are Buried in Debt," *New York Times*, May 28, 2010, www.nytimes.com/2010/05/29/your-money/student-loans/29money.html?src=me&ref=homepage. Excellent piece—and rowdy comments—on where the blame lies when college students/grads get too deep in debt.

Philip Oreopoulos and Kjell G. Salvanes, "How Large Are Returns to Schooling? Hint: Money Isn't Everything," National Bureau of Economic Research, September 2009, www.nber.org/papers/w15339. Paper on how the returns made on an education aren't just about money.

PayScale.com, "Best Undergrad College Degrees by Salary," www.payscale.com/best-colleges/degrees.asp. List of best-paying college degrees for 2010–2011.

Pew Research Center, "Are We Happy Yet?" February 13, 2006, http://pewresearch.org/assets/social/pdf/AreWeHappyYet.pdf. Study showing that college grads are "happier."

Richard Rothstein, "College Graduates: Supply and Demand," Economic Policy In-

stitute, July 21, 2009, www.epi.org/analysis_and_opinion/entry/college_gradu
ates_supply_and_demand. Great piece on the demand for college grads—it's
falling and why.

SavingforCollege.com. Part of Bankrate.com, this is a great site to compare and shop
for college savings plans, such as 529s and Coverdells.

Herwig Schlunk, "Mamas Don't Let Your Babies Grow Up to Be . . . Lawyers," Van-
derbilt University Law School, October 29, 2009, http://online.wsj.com/public/
resources/documents/SSRN-id1497044.pdf. Is it worthwhile to get a law degree?

U.S. Department of Education, "Federal Student Aid," http://studentaid.ed.gov.
Starting point for research/resources on federal grants, loans, and work-study
programs.

U.S. Department of Education, "Federal Student Aid: Repayment Information,"
http://studentaid.ed.gov/PORTALSWebApp/students/english/repaying.jsp. Information on federal loan repayment, programs for when you can't pay, and loan
forgiveness.

U.S. Department of Education, Institute of Education Sciences, National Center for
Education Statistics, http://nces.ed.gov.

The Real Cost of Bad Habits

American Heart Association, "Cigarette Smoking and Cardiovascular Diseases,"
www.americanheart.org/presenter.jhtml?identifier=4545. Smoking stats and
info.

American Heart Association, "Obesity and Nutrition Health Policy," www.american
heart.org/presenter.jhtml?identifier=3068641. News and links on the health
risks (especially vascular) of being overweight and obese.

American Lung Association, "State 'Smoker Protection' Laws," http://slati.lungusa
.org/appendixf.asp.

Jay Bhattacharya and Neeraj Sood, "Health Insurance, Obesity, and Its Economic
Costs," The Economics of Obesity, May 2004, www.ers.usda.gov/publications/
efan04004/efan04004g.pdf.

Centers for Disease Control and Prevention, "Overweight and Obesity," www.cdc
.gov/obesity. News and research.

Centers for Disease Control and Prevention, "Smoking and Tobacco Use," www.cdc
.gov/tobacco/data_statistics/index.htm. Reports and resources.

Chris Fleming, "Wellness Programs and Diabetes Costs," Health Affairs, January 14,
2010, http://healthaffairs.org/blog/2010/01/14/wellness-programs-and-diabetes

-costs. A leading journal of health policy thought and research; includes links to "Workplace Wellness Programs Can Generate Savings" and "The Economic Burden of Diabetes."

Michael F. Jacobson, "Petition to Require Health Messages on Soft Drinks Containing High-Fructose Corn Syrup and Other Caloric Sweeteners," Center for Science in the Public Interest, www.cspinet.org/new/pdf/final_soda_petition.pdf. Report on the harmful effects of soda consumption, submitted to the U.S. Department of Health and Human Services and the FDA.

James E. Kloeppel, "Weight Gain of U.S. Drivers Has Increased Nation's Fuel Consumption," *News Bureau*, University of Illinois, October 24, 2006, http://news .illinois.edu/news/06/1024auto.html.

National Cancer Institute, "Secondhand Smoke," www.smokefree.gov/topic-second hand_smoke.aspx. Effects of secondhand smoking.

National Highway Traffic Safety Administration, www.nhtsa.gov. Read up on all bad driving habits (including those of teen and senior drivers).

Michael Pollan, *The Omnivore's Dilemma: A Natural History of Four Meals* (New York: Penguin Press, 2006). Eye-opening book on the American food system with a look at obesity and the ubiquity of corn.

Rebecca M. Puhl and Chelsea A. Heuer, "The Stigma of Obesity: A Review and Update," *Obesity* 17, no. 5 (2009), www.yaleruddcenter.org/resources/upload/ docs/what/bias/WeightBiasStudy.pdf. A Yale University study on weight bias in the workplace.

U.S. Department of Transportation, "Statistics and Facts About Distracted Driving," www.distraction.gov/stats-and-facts.

Weight-Control Information Network, "Economic Costs Related to Overweight and Obesity," National Institute of Diabetes and Digestive and Kidney Diseases, www.win.niddk.nih.gov/statistics/index.htm#econ.

The Real Cost of Being Your Own Boss

Robert W. Fairlie, "Self-Employed Business Ownership Rates in the United States: 1979–2003," U.S. Small Business Administration, December 2004, www.sba.gov/ advo/research/rs243tot.pdf.

Freelancers Union, www.freelancersunion.org. Hub and union for freelancers with resources for lower-cost insurance coverage, filing legal claims, and networking.

LowerMyBills.com and BillShrink.com. Sites to find and get lower rates on home services such as cell, landline, and Internet access.

Rich Morin, "Take This Job and Love It," Pew Research Center, September 17, 2009, http://pewresearch.org/pubs/1346/self-employed-significantly-more-satisfied-with-jobs. Report finding that the self-employed are more satisfied with their jobs.

U.S. Department of Labor, Bureau of Labor Statistics, www.bls.gov/home.htm. Government home base for stats on the American workforce.

U.S. Department of Labor, "FAQs for Employees About COBRA Continuation Health Coverage," www.dol.gov/ebsa/faqs/faq_consumer_cobra.html.

U.S. Internal Revenue Service, "Small Business and Self-Employed Tax Center," www.irs.gov/businesses/small/index.html.

U.S. Small Business Administration, "Guaranteed Loan Programs," www.sba.gov/financialassistance/borrowers/guaranteed.

The Real Cost of Credit Cards

AnnualCreditReport.com. The *only* place to go once a year for your free credit reports from the three reporting agencies: Experian, Equifax, and Transunion.

Bankrate.com and LowCards.com. To compare credit card offers—note especially fees, just as much as interest rates.

Dinkytown.net. Not the prettiest site, but a cornucopia of financial calculators; the credit card pay-downs are some of the best.

Lucia F. Dunn and Ida Mirzaie, "Consumer Debt Stress Index Report," Ohio State University, September 2009, http://chrr.ohio-state.edu/content/surveys/cfm/debt/DSI_200909.pdf.

Federal Trade Commission, "Fair Debt Collection Practices Act," 2006, www.ftc.gov/bcp/edu/pubs/consumer/credit/cre27.pdf. The act that protects consumers from unfair, harassing debt collection. These are your rights.

MyFICO.com. Yes, there are many credit scores out there but the majority of lenders use your three FICO scores based on your credit reports.

National Foundation for Credit Counseling, www.nfcc.org. Great resource for help with credit and finding a nonprofit credit counselor near you.

U.S. Courts, "Bankruptcy," www.uscourts.gov/FederalCourts/Bankruptcy.aspx. A guide to bankruptcy basics, your options, and the legal process.

U.S. Federal Reserve, "Fair Debt Collection Practices Act," *Consumer Compliance Handbook*, January 2006, www.federalreserve.gov/boarddocs/supmanual/cch/fairdebt.pdf. A tad clearer breakdown of your rights.

U.S. Internal Revenue Service, "Publication 908: Bankruptcy Tax Guide," March

2009, www.irs.gov/publications/p908/index.html. Guide to bankruptcy, exemptions, and taxes.

The Real Cost of Saving

Bankrate.com. Yup, these guys again. Shop around for savings rates (and fees) at banks near you including community banks.

BillShrink.com, RetailMeNot.com, FatWallet.com, CouponMom.com, PriceGrabber.com. All great sites to make sure you don't pay retail and save more money.

Federal Deposit Insurance Corporation, www.fdic.gov. The government organization that insures our bank holdings. Find out if your bank has coverage and how coverage of your deposits works.

Federal Deposit Insurance Corporation, "Electronic Deposit Insurance Estimator (EDIE)," www.fdic.gov/edie/index.html. A tool to figure out what and how much of your money is covered—or not—under FDIC insurance rules.

National Credit Union Administration, www.ncua.gov. Credit unions tend to offer better rates on savings and CDs than commercial banks.

Wesabe.com and Geezeo.com. Great sites with free budgeting resources to help you save.

The Real Cost of Investing

David E. Adler, "The Disposition Effect," *NOVA*, PBS, March 1, 2010, www.pbs.org/wgbh/nova/body/adler-stocks.html. A clear examination of the disposition effect—how, why, and when we trade our investments.

Jack Bogle, *The Little Book of Common Sense Investing: The Only Way to Guarantee Your Fair Share of Stock Market Returns* (Hoboken, NJ: John Wiley & Sons, 2007). "Common sense" is so little used and applied to investing, how can you resist? I'm a fan.

Dinkytown.net, "Compare Investment Fees," www.dinkytown.net/java/CompareFees .html. Those Dinkytown guys again, this time allowing you to compare the "bite" of investing fees.

Financial Planning Association, www.fpanet.org. To find a fee-based financial planner.

Morningstar, "Mutual Fund Insights," www.morningstar.com/cover/funds.aspx. Compare mutual fund (including index fund) performances over time and view ratings.

National Association of Personal Financial Advisors, www.napfa.org. Another resource for finding a fee-based adviser.

Daniel R. Solin, *The Smartest Investment Book You'll Ever Read: The Simple, Stress-Free Way to Reach Your Investment Goals* (New York: Perigee, 2006).

StatTrek, "Statistics and Probability Tutorial: Introduction," http://stattrek.com/Lesson1/Statistics-Intro.aspx?Tutorial=Stat. Fun tutorials on probability and statistics.

U.S. Department of Labor, "Investing and Diversification," www.dol.gov/ebsa/investing.html. A primer on investing and the importance of diversification.

U.S. Securities and Exchange Commission, www.sec.gov. Investing information and the ability to research a financial planner, adviser, or broker's background and registration.

U.S. Securities and Exchange Commission, "Mutual Fund Fees and Expenses," www.sec.gov/answers/mffees.htm. An SEC primer on mutual fund management fees.

ACKNOWLEDGMENTS

A heartfelt gracias to my dearest Lawrence; to Laura ("Lola") Giannotti, dear sister, researcher, and fact-checker; to John Duff and Jeanette Shaw, editors extraordinaire; to Kris Dahl and ICM; my "OTM"ers (you know who you are); and to all the folks who watched and continue to watch, email, and friend me. I do it for you.

INDEX

Page numbers in *italics* represent charts.

Index